Further praise for *Finding the Words*

"*Finding The Words* is a one-of-a-kind treasure. It is a must-read for anyone navigating the often-tricky waters of effective and heartfelt conversations with loved ones. We all owe a debt of gratitude to Susan Halpern for bringing these inspiring stories and inspired principles into our lives. This book will save you countless hours of fear and frustration and maybe even a vital relationship or two."

—CHARLES A. GARFIELD, PHD, founder of Shanti and clinical professor of psychology, Department of Psychiatry, UCSF

"Challenging interactions and conversations are an inescapable part of life, but Susan Halpern's words and wisdom help us navigate them."

—ROGER WALSH, MD, PHD, professor of psychiatry, philosophy, and anthropology, University of California at Irvine and author of *Essential Spirituality: The Seven Central Practices*

"This book is a gift for anyone wanting to heal and deepen relationships at any stage of life. Susan Halpern's wisdom, experience, and the light of compassion shine through the words that show us how to release old patterns of behavior and open our hearts to more love in our lives."

—FRANCES VAUGHN, PHD, psychologist and author of *Shadows of the Sacred*

"Susan Halpern's second book turns out to be as valuable as her first, *The Etiquette of Illness*. I found *Finding the Words* to be an honest, open, and truthful aid in assisting individuals, families, and community members to find the necessary words to move through difficult life moments. I will keep this book on my desk as a reminder and a guide for those important life conversations with loved ones."

—PATRICIA DE JONG, senior minister, First Congregational Church of Berkeley

finding the words

finding the
words

candid conversations with
Loved Ones

SUSAN P. HALPERN, MSW

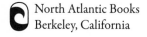 North Atlantic Books
Berkeley, California

Published by
North Atlantic Books
P.O. Box 12327
Berkeley, California 94712

Cover art © Peter Zelei/iStock
Cover and book design by Claudia Smelser
Printed in the United States of America

Finding the Words: Candid Conversations with Loved Ones is sponsored by the Society for the Study of Native Arts and Sciences, a nonprofit educational corporation whose goals are to develop an educational and cross-cultural perspective linking various scientific, social, and artistic fields; to nurture a holistic view of arts, sciences, humanities, and healing; and to publish and distribute literature on the relationship of mind, body, and nature.

North Atlantic Books' publications are available through most bookstores. For further information, visit our Web site at www.northatlanticbooks.com or call 800-733-3000.

Library of Congress Cataloging-in-Publication Data

Halpern, Susan P.
  Finding the words : candid conversations with loved ones / Susan P. Halpern.
    p. cm.
  Summary: "Offers readers practical suggestions and scripted solutions for discussing difficult issues—love, sex, money, divorce, aging—with partners, parents, children, and siblings"—Provided by publisher.
  ISBN 978-1-55643-838-7
  1. Interpersonal communication. 2. Communication in the family. 3. Conversation. I. Title.
  BF637.C45H2815 2009
  153.6–dc22   2009014674

1 2 3 4 5 6 7 8 9   Sheridan   14 13 12 11 10 09

*I dedicate this book to my children and grandchildren
with love and appreciation for the joy they bring to me.*

Acknowledgments

To begin this book, I needed to find a nurturing space and the time for deep reflection. I returned to the lake country north of Toronto, to the cottage of my friends Joy Davey and Lawrence Stibbard. On the shores of Lake Kabakwa, I began writing this book. On my return to Berkeley, with the support and expertise of Jane Anne Staw, my writing coach, I continued my work.

I am grateful to the staff of North Atlantic Books, who asked to see my book and then chose to publish it. Working with each of you has been a pleasure.

I want to thank the supervisors, mentors, and teachers from my thirty or more years as a psychotherapist. Each of you helped me to know myself and to believe in myself. My therapist friends have been helpful in many ways, particularly Lauren Friedman, Michael Pearlman, Susan Orr, Connie Holmes, Geri Rossen, Robert Gass, Judith Ansara Gass, Joy Davey, and Laurence Stibbard. I owe a special debt of gratitude to my friends who have talked to me about their perplexing lives and puzzled with me over what they did and might have done. I want to thank the people who gave generously of their time and personal experiences to help me understand specific issues in the book. I am grateful to them for discussing with me their life challenges, and for their insight and candor.

This book would not exist without my husband, Charlie, who has influenced my thinking, engaged with me through the years with love and acceptance, and read and reread this book with patience, enthusiasm, and a critical eye. My children, my grandchildren, and their spouses have taught me and supported me in my life, including and beyond this book. I thank you for being the caring sensitive people you are.

Contents

Introduction   I

CHAPTER 1

Cultivating Conscious Conversations as a Couple   5

What Can I Say When I Am Furious?   7
When Is It Time to Talk to My Partner?   9
All Husbands Take Out the Garbage. Why Don't You?   II
Why Is My Partner Always Trying to Fix My Problems?   12
How Can We Stop Having the Same Argument Over and Over?   13
Do All Conflicts Need to Be Resolved?   15
What If I Don't Want to Talk This Through?   15
Conclusion   17

CHAPTER 2

Getting Along in a Love Relationship   19

Can I Stick to My Plan to Speak with Kindness?   19
How Can I Find My Way to Loving Acceptance?   21
Do I Have to Tell You Everything?   22
Why Can't You Read My Mind?   24

Will Letting Out My Anger Make Things Worse? 25
How Can I End This Fight? 27
Why Is It So Hard to Say I'm Sorry? 29
Why Is It So Hard to Say Yes? 30
How Can I Say No and Not Hurt Him? 30
Conclusion 31

CHAPTER 3

Accepting Differences between Partners 33

Don't You Have Any Feelings? 33
Why Are You Always Late? 36
How Can We Find Our Way Back to Intimacy? 37
If Only We Had Been Candid about Our Differences 39
Why Can't We Ever Do What I Want? 41
How Can I Compromise When I Am So Afraid? 43
How Are We Going to Live Together
    After All These Years Apart? 45
Why Can't He Treat the Children the Way I Do? 48
Conclusion 51

CHAPTER 4

Bringing Words of Love to Intimate Moments 53

How Can I Learn to Say "I Love You"? 53
How Can We Keep Love Alive? 55
How Can I Talk about What Works for Me in Bed? 56
What Do People Say While Making Love? 59
How Can We Keep Sex Exciting? 60
How Can I Talk about My Sexual Attractions? 62
Can I Be Intimate without Sex? 64
Conclusion 65

CHAPTER 5

Speaking Candidly during a Major Life Crisis   67

Illness   67
How Can I Talk to Him about His Prostate Cancer?   68
How Can I Tell Him I Can't Meet All His Needs?   71
Substance Abuse   74
What Can I Do to Protect Myself from His Drinking?   75
Why Doesn't My Husband Care That I Drink?   76
Job Loss   77
How Do I Respond to You Losing Your Job?   78
How Can I Help My Partner with His Professional Difficulty? 79
Infidelity   81
Do I Have to End the Marriage?   81
How Can I Tell Him I Am Seeing Someone Else?   83
Can We Renegotiate the Conditions of Our Marriage?   85
Conclusion   86

CHAPTER 6

Making Divorce Less Disruptive and Painful   87

I Can't Remember Why I Married This Person   88
What Am I Going to Say to End This Marriage?   89
What Will It Take to Forgive?   90
How Will We Tell Our Parents   91
Please Let Me Tell Our Friends When I Am Ready   94
Can a Divorce Be Peaceful?   95
How Can We Work Together
to Prepare the Children for Our Divorce?   97
What Should We Say to the Children?   98
What Do I Tell the Children about My Love Life?   99
Will the Children Ever Talk about the Divorce with Me?   100

Even Though I Am Forty,
I Want to Know Why My Parents Divorced 101
How Can I Reach Out to My Children Years after My Divorce? 103
Conclusion 104

CHAPTER 7

Learning to Be Adults with Each Other—
Parents and Adult Children 107

How Can I Get My Son to Talk to Me? 108
Why Do They Tell Me These Things? 110
Why Does My Daughter Talk More to Her Aunt Than to Me? 112
What Can I Say When My Adult Child Is Angry with Me? 113
How Can I Get My Parents to Listen to How I Am Feeling? 114
How Does a Mother Ask for What She Wants? 115
When Do Daughters Get to Express Their Need 116
How Can I Get More from My Father? 118
How Do I Handle My Disapproval of My Daughter? 120
How Can I Help My Adult Children Talk to Each Other? 122
Conclusion 124

CHAPTER 8

Watching Married Children Find Their Own Way 125

How Can I Ask My Mother for Help? 125
What Can I Say to My Father about His Broken Promises? 127
What Is a Mother-in-Law's Business? 129
What Can I Say When My Parents
Tell Me How to Raise My Children? 130
How Do I Learn to Be a Good In-Law? 132
How Can We Help Our Child Through Divorce? 134
How Long Should I Give Financial Support? 136
Conclusion 138

CHAPTER 9

Repairing a Rift between Parents and an Adult Child   141

What Is Going On When an Adult Child Breaks Off
from His or Her Family?   141
What Can I Say about My Need for Time Away?   143
What Might Parents Ask When They Want
to Understand Their Child's Absence?   144
How Can I Reconnect with My Father?   145
How Can I Reconnect with My Son?   149
How Can I Get My Whole Family Together Again?   151
What Will We Talk About When We Meet?   153
Conclusion   155

CHAPTER 10

Supporting Adult Children as They Begin to Parent   157

Who Gets to Name the Baby?   158
How Do I Respond to My Children's Questions?   159
Is It Okay to Speak Up for Health?   160
Is It Okay to Speak Up for Safety?   161
How Can I Choose between a Child and a Grandchild?   163
How Can I Help?   164
How Can Grandparents Find Ways to Help, Not Hinder?   166
Can Grandparents Write Different Rules for Their House?   167
How Can Grandparents Talk about Their Needs?   168
How Can I Make Relocating Nearer to My Children
and Grandchildren Work for All of Us?   170
What Should I Do If My Children
Do Not Invite Me to Relocate?   172
Conclusion   173

CHAPTER 11

Nurturing and Reviving Friendships among Siblings 175

What Should I Say When I Disagree with My Sibling's Politics? 176
How Can I Reach Out to a Sibling? 177
How Can I Reach Out to a Sibling I No Longer Know? 179
How Can I Get Along with My Sister-in-Law? 180
How Can Two Sisters Support Their Aging Aunt? 181
How Do I Handle My Brother's Misuse of Drugs and Money? 183
Should I Confront My Sister about Her Drinking? 185
How Can We Fairly Divide the Estate? 186
Should I Invite My Brother to Live with Me
    during His Divorce? 188
Do I Have to Welcome My Sister-in-Law into My Marriage? 191
Conclusion 192

CHAPTER 12

*Using Intergenerational Conversations
to Make Decisions at the End of Life* 193

Will I Make a Timely Decision to Stop Driving? 194
How Can I Convince My Elderly Parents to Stop Driving? 195
When Should I Visit My Aging Mother
    Who Lives in Another State? 200
How Can I Convince My Parents to Accept Outside Help? 202
How Can I Care for My Wife When She Is a Reluctant Patient? 205
How Can I Help My Mother Move to a Senior Residence? 207
What Is Happening to This Body of Mine? 210
Should I Invite My Mother to Live with Us? 212
How Do I Tell Someone I Love That Her Memory Is Failing? 214
How Do I Talk to a Person with Alzheimer's Disease? 215
When Should I Write My Will? 217

CONTENTS

How Am I Going to Make Decisions for My Father?   219
How Should I Make Decisions
   When My Loved One Is Unresponsive?   221
How One Family Let Mother Go into Death   222
Conclusion   224

Afterword   227

Introduction

When my mother was eighty-eight, I realized that I needed to talk to her about not driving anymore. Although I was not sure it was time for her to stop driving, I wanted to open the conversation. At the time we lived in different cities, so I waited until my next visit. On our way to the restaurant where we had planned to have dinner, she barely missed hitting a car. I was shaken and frightened. I wanted to proceed with tact, but instead I blurted out, "I think you need to stop driving. You nearly hit that car."

"I did not, and I am not ready," my mother retorted sharply.

Realizing I had done more damage than good, I stopped the conversation. I had let myself down and humiliated my mother. My tone of voice as well as the words I used must have felt to her like an attack. Now I wanted to run away from the topic and never bring it up again.

I returned home baffled about what to do, and learned many of my friends were dealing with the same issue. They talked to me about the ways they resolved this issue with their parents. They reminded me how sensitive an area driving is, and that I must let my mother know I recognize the painfulness of this life change. I began to think about what I might have done differently.

The driving issue with my mother started me thinking about difficult conversations with loved ones in a variety of situations. How to formulate sentences, when to speak, when not to speak—

all require consideration, love, and empathy. I thought about the many moments in personal relationships that would improve with preparation.

My thoughts then turned to my marriage of close to fifty years, which, with time, has gained in strength and richness. Yet my husband and I still tangle over petty comments, get caught by different expectations, and become angry over minor differences of opinion. Over the years we have had time to try out many ways to respond to these moments: mitigation, resolve, letting go, and even laughter. When I looked back at the principles, practices, and techniques that we have used in our moments of strife, I realize that the negative moments still come, but less often, less intense, and for a shorter duration.

I have written this book to offer ways to ride in the river of love, nourished by the waters, able to deal with the rocks, rapids, and twists as we move through our lives. My advice is based on my training and practice of psychotherapy for over thirty years, my own life experiences, and the stories of my clients, friends, and children.

In my 2003 book, *The Etiquette of Illness: What to Say When You Can't Find the Words,* I offered words for caregivers and patients to use with each other when illness dominated their interaction. From the letters and e-mails I received, I found that some readers like having actual words and phrases available to them in moments when they want to speak but are fearful they might "get it wrong." Again I offer examples that minimize the details of the internal struggle, focusing instead on the principles of communication and suggested words to use while maintaining and often enhancing the relationship. Of course, these are only suggestions, points of departure. My suggestions can be used as they are or revised according to your particular situation and the loved ones involved.

In *Finding the Words: Candid Conversations with Loved Ones,* I describe situations in which people speak honestly to their loved ones, from the heart, with care and decency, and from a place of conscious thought. I discourage rushing in headlong and exploding with unexamined emotion. I encourage choosing a place, a time, and words of consideration and kindness when you want to preserve and nourish a relationship, yet understand the importance of speaking your mind. While differences and disharmony are inevitable, using the tools offered here will help you avoid the most toxic confrontations, shorten the recovery period after an unavoidable family crisis, and bring understanding and even forgiveness to your relationships.

Finding the Words: Candid Conversations with Loved Ones describes moments in which we speak the truth and allow ourselves to be vulnerable in order to diffuse tension and move a relationship toward comfort and love. The book offers principles and practices to help us find our words—with partners, ex-partners, children before and after divorce, in-laws, parents, siblings, adult children, and grandchildren. I describe tensions that occur and how conversations might be conducted to reduce harm. Anger will still erupt. Words will fly. Voices will rise. Rage will seethe, inside and outside. That is part of being in relationship with another people. Here I offer ways to hear the issues arising; slow down the reactivity; find the words to reengage with peace, love, and acceptance; and return to harmony.

During this time of economic uncertainty, it is especially important to bring awareness into charged conversations with family members. As the economic downturn affects our lives, new issues will surface in our close relationships. Couples may have to discuss what to do to simplify their lifestyle or find new jobs. Parents may have to decide how to help their unemployed adult children. Siblings may have to talk about how much financial help they can give their aging parents. The processes described here will help you cope with some challenging new issues and a higher degree of stress.

The principles discussed and illustrated in *Finding the Words* are useful in all relationships—within a family as well as in life outside the family. All the chapters, therefore, are useful, not just the one that addresses your immediate concerns. The stakes are high in loving relationships. We want to be in each other's lives for a long time. Moving past the negative moments and exchanges takes conscious effort.

The book sets the stage for you to find your own way in the sometimes murky waters of relationships so you can achieve satisfying rapport. For forgiveness to be a possibility, for respect and affection to enter a discordant conversation, we must be responsible for our own words and deeds. By setting our intentions to bring an open, caring heart and words of respect and candor to all our relationships, we can each be a catalyst for love and peace. Beneath all the noise of daily living and interacting, we can nurture the bonds of love that sustain and enrich our lives.

The experiences described in this book are drawn from real life and are often the merging of one or more stories to create a point. The real names and identities are disguised for purposes of confidentiality. If anyone in the book reminds you of yourself, it is because the examples are based on real people.

CHAPTER I

Cultivating Conscious Conversations as a Couple*

Love is the most fulfilling human experience. We hear that message from philosophers, theologians, therapists, seekers, and people who have had a near-death experience. Love is valued highly in our culture. We seek it, we bask in it, and yet it can be so evanescent, as though it might fly out the window any moment. Learning how to move a relationship out of conflict and back to comfort is a work in progress. We can learn to watch our emotions rise and then fall. We can feel love subside and then rise again. Emotions are not permanent; they will arise and pass and arise again. What matters is how we deal with our feelings. Let's hold the big picture in mind: that love endures underneath the daily ups and downs, that love heals and connects us, that love is the essence of human experience. Now the pertinent questions arise: How can we build, maintain, and enhance our loving connections? How can we let go of our need to win and our righteous indignation? How can we return to our heart?

Love is the underlying stratum we can learn to return to in times of differences and distress. Intimacy, trust, and respect rise and fall. Joy, sorrow, and anger come and go. Rage and resentment have their

*Note: I use the word *couple* as shorthand to refer to any peer, long-term, committed love relationship, regardless of gender, living arrangements, or license.

moments. Holding love as a flowing, unending river that runs through our lives will allow us to flourish and grow in our relationships. Couple interactions are ever changing in nature. Periods of loving conversation and easy discourse may be followed by sharp remarks or silence, or both. Each couple has its own way of returning to calm. Inside the conversations, the wordless exchanges, and the coping with day-to-day events, each couple experiences shifting levels of intimacy, a variety of conversations, and numerous ways of resolving differences. Ideally, loving is a continuum underneath the daily noise.

To reach the goal of sustaining a loving connection, we need to listen to our partner with interest, curiosity, and an open heart, in a way that allows us to hear our loved one's point of view, intentions, and values. Then we can recognize the importance of his or her position, empathize, and respond with less attachment to our own position. Conversations that lead to understanding can take many forms, and may be different during a conflict than before and after. Listening fully and speaking with awareness allows for negotiation, compromise, forgiveness, and compassion. By bringing consciousness and a loving heart to our interactions, the hyperbole, high drama, and hurtful words have a better chance of being replaced by kindness, equanimity, and resolution.

A relationship that is intimate includes trust, love, devotion, respect, tolerance, acceptance, delight, surprise, letting go, speaking the truth, a soul connection, and laughter. *Couple-hood* includes an interest in each other's doings and thinking; respect for each other's work, interests, talents, and abilities; and delight in each other's *differentness* and *sameness*. Couples have ups and downs—days of anger, nights of silence, fights, disagreements, yelling, and making up. To return to respect and love takes talk, compromise, negotiation, and flexibility. How do we keep alive the love that exists beneath

6

the day-to-day commotion? How do we keep a loving connection that will sustain us for a lifetime?

Couples move out of conflict and back to harmony in many different ways. Some couples rise early to talk, cuddle, and giggle. Other couples meditate together in the cold in a hut by the Pacific Ocean, or jog up a mountainside in Massachusetts. Some couples love to travel together, shop together, explore caves together, talk about their children, garden, kayak, party, go to galleries and art shows; they thoroughly enjoy doing things together. Other couples spend most of their time apart and then love coming together to talk about their experiences. Each couple works out its own degree of interdependence and interaction. When the distance and closeness are satisfactory to both members, the relationship is working well, their intimate connection is maintained. To establish, maintain, and enhance the intimacy that nourishes love, couples need to have ways to resolve their differences. They need to consciously set their intentions, and in so doing they need to support each other.

What Can I Say When I Am Furious?

Anger erupts with no forethought. It is not patient or polite. It flies out. Words are shouted, plates may sail across the room, feet stamp, hands gesture, eyes blaze, and faces contort. Revenge, righteousness, resentment, historic wrongs, harsh words, sarcasm, and cold shoulders fill the space. Anger is difficult to stop when it is blowing hard. When anger subsides, new questions arise: How can I return to being my loving self? What can I say afterward and how can I get past the anger, sullenness, and silence?

The aggressor has a moment before the attack, or anytime during the attack, to take a breath and retreat. Likewise, the responder to the attack can pause and look inward to consider different choices before reacting. This is where consciousness and control come into play. Remember that you have options.

- Do I want to escalate?
- I want to diffuse?
- I want to be calmly honest with my partner and myself?
- I want to be understood. How can I achieve that?

A four-step process for *complete communication* requires stating our thoughts, our feelings, our intentions, and our plan of action. This may sound formulaic at first, but by reviewing in our mind these four steps, we can clearly communicate to our partner, revealing ourselves in a way that can lead to mutual understanding.

1. The thought: I don't want to be angry.
2. The feeling: I am furious that she treats me like this.
3. The intention: I want this to go well for both of us.
4. The plan of action: I am going to speak about my desire to talk reasonably.

Stating your full range of thoughts, feelings, intentions, and action plans opens the possibility of a similar reply from the other person. In the face of continued rage, hold onto your desire to move toward understanding. The hardest moment is shifting the tone from anger to neutrality. Sometimes you have to state your intention a few times. If that does not work, leave the field. Wait until the fury has cooled and a conversation can take place. On returning you might say:

- Is this a good time to talk about what happened?
- I would like us to talk in a way that allows us to move forward, and have fewer exchanges like that again. Are you interested in doing that?
- I love you. I want to connect to you first, before we undertake this difficult conversation.

* I feel that my part in the conflict was ... [stated from a place of responsibility, not from the stance of a victim].

You can ask and listen, let go, compromise, negotiate, own your own part in the problem, acknowledge your underlying fears, and, finally, even laugh and touch.

When Is It Time to Talk to My Partner?

When you find yourself having a mental conversation, or talking with a friend or therapist, and you find yourself defending your position and blaming your partner, then you need to think about which needs of yours are not being met and how you might address the subject without starting an argument. You can remind yourself that you need to talk about your grievances rather than saving them up and thinking your displeasure will pass. If something is bothering you, you need to open the subject. If you wait for your partner to raise the subject, nothing will be said. This is a chance to take responsibility for yourself.

Planning when and where to have a difficult conversation makes a difference. Ask, "When would be a good time to talk about x?" This gives the other person some control, and allows him to start to think about x before you come to him with your position. This gives him the opportunity to prepare. He might respond, "I will get back to you after I have thought this through."

When the time comes to talk, sit in a comfortable place. Choose the time so you won't be interrupted. Slow down, breathe, face your partner.

Keep in mind that you can't demand change. You can only speak of what is not working for you, acknowledge your part in the problem, and say what you are willing to do about it. When you are working cooperatively, with openness to the other person's perspective, there is a chance that a solution or resolution will arise—if not immediately, then soon.

Raising the subject of household responsibilities might go like this:

1. The thought: I want to talk to you about the sharing of responsibilities. I am hoping you will take on some of the jobs that serve us both.

2. The feeling: I find I am angry quite often about the way we divide up the household tasks.

3. The intention: I want to stop criticizing you. I want this conversation to go well for both of us.

4. The plan of action: I will try to stop criticizing you about they way you help. I will express my gratitude for your helping.

With interest and curiosity, listen to your partner's response. Then, with sincerity, thank your partner for listening and working on this with you.

Conversations on charged subjects take planning, clarity, and a welcoming tone of voice. Complete communication may take several tries; it may take several months for the practices to change. But if you don't talk about your anger, it builds and builds, and if your partner does not know you are raging inside, she cannot know that you need to talk and adjust some behaviors. Only by putting words to your thoughts, feelings, intentions, and plans can you give your partner an opportunity to help find a solution that suits both of you. Connecting with love at the start and at the conclusion is valuable. When each person feels heard and understood, and when both feel better than when they began, the conversation is successful. Treat even a little learning and a return to neutrality as a success, then congratulate your partner and acknowledge the sincere effort.

All Husbands Take Out the Garbage.
Why Don't You?

Evelyn, a shy young woman, had trouble stating her needs and expectations to Alex, her new husband. Even asking him to take the garbage out to the street felt to her like nagging. Over time she became so annoyed with taking out the garbage that she said to Alex, "All husband's take out the garbage."

This did not move Alex. He continued to read the newspaper.

Evelyn thought about the situation for a bit, then realized that what she needed to say was, "I would like you to take out the garbage." But Evelyn was reluctant to use the first person pronoun; she felt it would make her sound demanding and pushy. However, the more Evelyn thought about it, the more she knew she had to change the way she expressed her desires.

As she began to feel comfortable using "I" when speaking to Alex, he too took more care to speak for himself, saying "I" instead of "You should" and "You could." Evelyn found that by using the first person pronoun she also began to voice opinions, ideas, hopes, and dreams. She began to feel stronger in herself without feeling strident. She began to own her pain and her joy. Her emotional range expanded. She felt herself take responsibility for her thoughts, ideas, and beliefs.

As the relationship developed between Evelyn and Alex, they learned to disagree, to confront, and to be angry because they were speaking accurately about themselves. They could only have untangled the "who did what to whom" that goes on with couples by using the correct pronouns and learning to speak of "what I am angry about" rather than "what you did." This formulation took the blame out of the angry statement and made each of them responsible for their own experience in the moment. They could recognize when the other was making assumptions that were invalid and state their true position or feelings.

Many people suffer from Evelyn's fear of speaking about herself in the first person. I met with a young woman, Tianna, who was a singer with a band. Onstage she had a huge personality, getting the audience to sing along, engaging with the other members of the band, reaching all the way to the back row with her voice. But she felt it was impossible to speak to her husband, a band member, in the privacy of their apartment about herself and her feelings. The first time I asked her to tell me about herself, she cried. No one had ever asked her to do that before. With my permission and modeling, Tianna learned to speak about herself in the first person, and then to speak about herself to her husband. Coming out from behind the anonymity of "you," "everyone," and "one," and speaking for yourself can be a huge step. In moments of anxiety or insecurity, even people who are fully connected to their own positions will revert to the impersonal "you" or "one" when "I" would make them feel uncomfortable.

Why Is My Partner Always Trying to Fix My Problems?

Lester felt inadequate, he realized, when Judy aired her personal concerns. He did not know what to do or say. His impulse was to think up a solution right away. All Judy wanted from Lester was that he listen when she talked about herself. He did not need to fix anything.

This is a common problem in relationships: When one person talks about a problem, the other thinks he is supposed to fix it. Only by telling our partner what we want can the need be met. Judy realized that she only wanted to be listened to. That was it. She wanted to hear herself talk through her issues, maybe get a little sympathy, and she would be fine. Lester did not need to do or say anything. If Lester said, "That sounds hard," that was sufficient.

When Lester came up with his great ideas, Judy felt he was saying she was dumb for not thinking of them herself. She felt belittled and dependent. He was the only one who could fix things, she felt. And often Lester's ideas were ones that Judy had entertained but found they did not fit. She did not want to keep saying no to his great ideas, but they weren't what she wanted from him. When she told him that she just needed time to talk and a friendly ear, she felt better and she went on to handle her problems in her own way. Judy had to tell Lester that she just wanted him to listen, and he learned to do just that.

How Can We Stop Having the Same Argument Over and Over?

Marvin and Polly are having the same fights now that they had forty years ago, when they were twenty and met in college, and neither of them has enjoyed fighting. They want to stop. As their fortieth anniversary approaches, Polly laments that they are still pulling at each other the same old way. In a calm period, they both decided to come up with ways to break through their typical power struggles, where each wants to get their own way. They are hoping for more consensual decision making and more gentleness. Polly says she cares more about the relationship than about being right. This is a key step. By separating the issues of the conflict and recognizing the value of the relationship, they could find a new way to cut through the old process with a few simple sentences.

- Here we are again, doing our usual dance, the I-want-it-my-way dance.
- I can't believe after all these years we are still doing this number.
- I am tired of this. I don't want to do it any more.
- I will do what you want because I feel like pleasing you today.

- I will do what you want this time, and I hope we can do what I want next time.
- Can you agree to that?
- How was this conversation for you?

If one partner makes the effort to name the dance in an amusing and neutral way, that can help both people move out of the old behavior patterns. Recognizing a pattern as it arises allows couples to cut through the old behavior into something new.

Here are a few typical patterns:

- The *dance-away person* wants distance from the partner.
- The *chaser* demands contact.
- The *clown* uses humor to avoid a discussion of what is going on.
- The *ostrich* denies that anything is going on.
- *Poor me* takes a victim stance to get his or her way.
- The *opera star* oppresses with high drama.
- The *yappy dog* keeps talking until the other gives in.
- The *rollover dog* gives in.
- The *contrarian,* who feels that agreement is passive, looks for disagreement.

By finding or creating the terms to describe their process, Polly and Marvin began to pull out of their repetitive patterns and find ways to enjoy each other in peace.

When the same old argument and discontent arise over and over, the process described in the first section of this chapter can be another way to let go.

- Choose a time and place conducive to a quiet conversation.
- Let go of being right and blaming.
- Approach each other with a loving, open, interested, and curious mind.
- Explore each other's underlying process.

- Acknowledge your own part in the problem.
- Speak about your thoughts, feelings, intentions, and plan of action.
- Thank each other and be pleased with yourselves.

Sometimes, understanding, acceptance, and compassion will flow, allowing you to let go of old patterns, assumptions, and grievances. Often there will be some positive movement, and the process can be repeated with benefits that continue to evolve and build.

Do All Conflicts Need to Be Resolved?

No. Not all disagreements, fights, and conflicts need to be resolved. Not all fights need to end with "I'm sorry." There are many ways to imply "I am sorry." Not all fights need to end with promises of better behavior in the future. Sometimes simply ending the spiral of negativity is enough to move on. Changing the subject or using a pleasant voice can bring us back to our best selves.

Some people find it is easy to say, "I apologize." Others offer their apologies by a hug or by moving away from an irresolvable moment. Getting in touch with what I did that may have played a part in the conflagration, instead of focusing on what he did that enraged me, is a more likely way to find a path to peace. Offering an apology for that part of the interchange for which I am truly sorry turns the conversation in a positive direction.

I am happier going through my day in a state of peace and love rather than anger, so it is worth it to me to work it out. No one ever really wins a fight: If someone wins, we both lose.

What If I Don't Want to Talk This Through?

Conscious conversation is not always the road to resolution. Stacy realized she needed to work on herself. Stacy loved Walter. They had an easy, flowing relationship that was interrupted by the way he left his clothes all over the bedroom for days—until Stacy yelled at him, nagged at him, and finally hung them up for him. Walter knew if he waited long enough, Stacy would tidy up. Stacy felt that Walter knew she hated the clothes all over the chair and the rack, sometimes even on the floor, so why would he not want to please her by picking them up? But he did not.

She tried hanging up the clothes without nagging. She tried writing him an e-mail on this subject. She asked him if he noticed when the bedroom was untidy. But nothing worked. Finally Stacy decided that it was not worth filling the air around them with annoyance; she would not talk to him about his mess anymore.

Clothes laying around had become Stacy's issue, and Walter seemed to float through it all without a thought. Stacy began to examine her need for order. Yes, it was her bedroom too, and she liked it a certain way, but she also liked her marriage to be peaceable. She could not have both if she held onto her anger. Stacy listened closely to her own process and asked herself over and over, "What happens when I see Walter's clothes lying around?" And she listened to her answers, going deeper and deeper.

- I am annoyed just looking at his socks on the floor.
- I am frustrated by his unwillingness to do this for me.
- I think he does not care about our room.
- I feel like his servant.
- I feel he has stopped caring.
- I am afraid I am losing him.
- I feel he does not love me when I see his socks on the floor.

Stacy's deepest fear was that Walter did not love her, but that was clearly not the case. In so many ways he showed her he loved her very much. He often picked up groceries; he helped with the cooking; he did all the laundry; he emptied and filled the dishwasher.

All tasks were equally shared. He told her he loved her; he treated her lovingly. Stacy realized that she was equating socks on the floor with lack of love. That was *her* issue, not Walter's issue. From this recognition, she worked to let go of her misapprehension and to focus on how Walter showed his love. Stacy decided she could pick up in the bedroom. She was good at it, she noticed the socks, so it was a good job for her. And Walter never complained about her picking up.

We all have many idiosyncrasies that turn into rubbing points in a committed relationship. Some can be changed; some cannot. Wisdom arises when we determine what can be left alone and just accepted. To reach that state of acceptance takes the work of self-examination, perhaps to recognize that a messy bedroom is not related to the absence of love. Stacy let go of her anger. She was able to move out of her feelings of anger by finding that underneath the anger was fear. She was afraid of not being loved. Recognizing the irrationality of this fear allowed her to let go of her demand for neatness without a conversation.

Conclusion

Couples who love each other are fun to be around. Their glow fills the room, their family, and their community. In an evolving relationship, conflict, resentment, annoyance, and anger can be brought up, looked at, sometimes even learned from—and then let go. Learning to speak and listen with the warmth of affection, attention, and humor, while allowing each other to be the person he or she is, keeps the relationship growing and strong.

CHAPTER 2

Getting Along in a Love Relationship

As couple-hood progresses, the itches and irritations that occur can be seen like riffles in the river of love, diverting us from the ease and calm of the flow, pushing us into backwaters, raising anxiety, and moving us off course. In this chapter, using examples of couples caught in the rapids, we will learn ways to get back into calm water.

Can I Stick to My Plan to Speak with Kindness?

Tom and Sal had a difficult marriage. They had very different attitudes about people, religion, and politics. At first intrigued by their differences, they later became annoyed. They disagreed sharply, often ended up yelling at each other and going to bed in silence. Each wanted the other to take the first step toward reconciliation.

One day, Tom talked with a friend over lunch. In answering his friend's questions, he had to reduce the blaming and recognize that some of the problem lay at his feet. When he began to see the relationship through his friend's eyes, he could no longer put all the blame on Sal's shoulders. Tom thought about how he treated Sal in the morning as they dressed for work, in the evening when they reunited at home, and when they were with their friends. He saw himself as petulant and recalcitrant. Tom heard the tone of his voice in his own head and did not like what he heard. He realized that he needed to change his tone and open his heart to Sal. He realized he needed to improve his interactions in order to feel better about himself as a spouse. He decided he would not make these changes to get Sal to do anything, but for himself.

Tom told Sal that he was going to try to be nice to her in order to improve their relationship, and he told her he hoped she would notice. He began by greeting her pleasantly, making time for her in the evening, and speaking nicely to her. As the days went by, he gave himself credit for softening toward Sal. He was proud of what he was doing. He stopped jumping on Sal when she was sharp, and he found being around her was getting easier.

At first, Sal was flummoxed. She did not know what was going on. She found it hard to believe Tom could come around to decency just like that. She distrusted his new way of speaking to her. She held onto her anger, which was stored up from all the years he had hurt her with his brusque, sarcastic comments. Tom began to apologize when he spoke sharply to her, and Sal began to feel a slight softening in her heart, but she found it difficult to be generous to Tom. She hung onto her anger. She could not get over her fear of being hurt. With time, as Tom stuck to his new manner even in the face of her resistance, Sal became ashamed of how she was acting. She decided to give being nice a try. She, too, began to speak nicely, expressed appreciation for Tom's change, and touched Tom more often. Through these simple and courageous steps, Sal and Tom slowly and unevenly found their way back to respect and kindness. They even learned to talk about sensitive subjects with curiosity and openness, instead of defensiveness and rigidity.

Tom undertook a major change without agreement from Sal. He decided he needed to do what he could to make the relationship a positive experience for both of them. He started by behaving in a way that allowed him to respect himself and, in the end, his new behavior was respectful of Sal too. Sal picked up the new language and began to move toward Tom. One reason change could happen was Tom's willingness to take action on his own, not as a manipulation to get Sal to change. He never asked her to be different. She, too, changed on her own—slowly, but she did change. By remaining true to his plan, Tom was able to feel good about himself and, ultimately, to feel good about Sal.

How Can I Find My Way to Loving Acceptance?

Sheila noted that any time she had a free moment her mind turned to her resentment against Greg. She kept a running list in her head of the times when he was brusque, when he failed to do things he said he would, when he put her down in public, and when he talked too much.

One day Sheila decided she was blaming Greg for everything and she should look instead at *her* behavior that irritated *him*. Upon reflection she realized Greg had told her that he did not like her interrupting, undermining his decisions, and being self-righteous about her calm exterior. She knew she humiliated him for his inability to find things in the refrigerator. As Sheila was able to see herself through Greg's eyes, she realized that she had a lot of improving to do on herself. She decided that instead of focusing on her husband's failures, she would look at her own behavior that might be interfering with the happiness of their relationship. All she could do, she concluded, was be the best person she could be, and try let go of her critical judgment of Greg. The word *judgment* caught her attention. If she stopped judging Greg and accepted him as he was, she would not have a list of grievances against him.

Sheila asked herself: Do I want an easy, loving relationship with myself and with Greg? Do I want a mind filled with happiness or a mind filled with resentment? Do I want to find out what I might think about if I'm not keeping track of his failures? What would it take to get there? Sheila decided to talk with Greg about her way of treating him. "I am sorry that at times I treat you badly. I want to stop. I have to learn to be kind and accepting. I hope you will be gentle with me when I talk harshly to you. I hope you will appreciate my effort." Sheila hoped that her acceptance of Greg would allow him to soften toward her.

Greg responded quickly: "Thank you for saying these things. I have been hard on you too. I want to stop this badgering we do with each other."

Their eyes filled with tears. They told each other how much they loved each other. They remembered to say that they would not be perfect all the time. They agreed to talk about their pent-up resentment as a way of healing the wounds. They hugged and agreed this felt like a breakthrough.

By admitting her own role in their challenging interactions, Sheila was able to open a difficult subject with Greg and move to a new place—a place that gave her space in her head to live her life with acceptance, and room in her heart to love her husband and forgive herself.

Do I Have to Tell You Everything?

Zenia and Harold learned the hard way that even though their marriage had a satisfying degree of openness and intimacy, not every thought or action needed to be shared. Every question did not need an answer.

Harold developed a crush on a woman in his office. He knew he would not be able to act on his feelings. He knew she would not have an affair with him, yet he was drawn to her. He found ways to work on projects with her. He loved going to work in the morning. Choosing his tie and socks while thinking about lunch in the common room with her was titillating. He sang as he dressed.

Zenia began to tease Harold, saying with laughter that he appeared to be dressing up for someone. He told her she was right, and he even named the woman. He hoped that by speaking lightly and including Zenia in his pleasure, she would feel good with him. Zenia, however, was hurt to discover that the light remark she had made was true. Old feelings of jealousy came up for her. She was angry with him for looking at another woman. He felt intruded upon. He was sorry he answered her question.

The light, open, easy exchange between Zenia and Harold might have worked for some couples, making them feel closer. Some couples do like to discuss their attractions to others, as long as each of them knows they are safe from betrayal. They find their partner's fantasies pleasurable. For other couples, the exclusiveness of the relationship does not leave room for this kind of feeling toward another. Even a casual verbal exchange on the subject can be damaging, leaving one partner feeling betrayed and the other confined.

Every couple has certain subjects that are better left unexplored between them, no matter how intimate their relationship. One woman finds she would rather not know about her husband's business decisions. A man knows he cannot criticize his wife's mother. Another couple knows they cannot discuss religion anymore. They each pray in their own way in separate churches.

Rather than assuming some subjects must be avoided in conversation, and rather than feeling left out and angry about some secretive areas of a partner's life, a couple can list the taboo subjects and openly acknowledge that they are to be avoided. The conversation to determine the areas that are off limits might sound like this:

- I find that when we talk about [mother, money, attractions, business, religion] the conversation goes nowhere and one of us gets angry.
- Let's agree not to talk about x.
- What topics do you want to keep to yourself?

• I would rather you did not offer your opinion about *y*.

For some of the off-limit subjects, a less stringent approach might be to say, "If I ask you a direct question, I would like you to answer. Otherwise, I will stay out of that territory. Can you agree to that?" If your partner agrees, then abide by the decision. Alternately, some couples may agree not to ask direct questions about taboo subjects.

Recognizing that each of us needs to have some things, though not too many, that are our own to do or to think about in our own way is an important aspect of respect in a working relationship. Respecting a few areas of our partner's privacy is part of the trust we establish in an intimate relationship, and this respect can make the rest of the conversations we have with our partner even richer and more binding. Of course if the list is long or one person does not feel comfortable respecting the silence of a partner on some topics, the idea of an agreement about privacy may not work.

Why Can't You Read My Mind?

Lana told me she was worn out waiting for Ronald to understand her. She did not want to tell him what was on her mind; she felt he should know her needs without telling him. She felt she could intuit what he wanted, but he had no idea what she wanted. She knew when to leave him alone and when to be near him, but he did not know when she wanted a simple foot massage or a cup of tea or a hug, and she felt cheated. He seriously misunderstood her need for his support after her mother became ill. Lana first wanted to go alone to visit with her mother. Then, when her mother died, she wanted Ronald with her. He got it all backwards, so she was alone at the funeral, a time when she needed him the most.

Lana would try to signal her wishes nonverbally, but Ronald did not fulfill them. When I asked Ronald if he felt he had worked hard to please Lana, he looked at me quizzically. I asked him what he thought her needs were. He did not know. He did think that at times she wanted something of him, but he admitted that he was not able to read her thoughts or even to guess when his support was needed.

As he heard Lana talk about how she could read his mind, Ronald became aware that she was not always on target, and that he had never corrected her. In fact, the idea of her reading him accurately made him feel taken over. He felt like a small, wordless being who needed a guide. As a result, what he wanted was to experience his own autonomy. By not even attempting to intuit her needs, he felt he was offering her the sense of personal space he wanted. Neither had explained their motivation to their partner.

As Lana began learning to put her desires into words, Ronald took a chance and began refining her "readings" of him, telling her what he was actually thinking and feeling instead of acting as though her guesses were correct. Lana began working on stating her wishes instead of hoping Ronald would guess what she needed from him. And she began to ask him out loud, not in the form of a demand but with curiosity, "I would like to know what you would like from me now?" She found it very hard at first; she felt pushy. But as a result, Ronald learned to answer Lana. By putting their desires and intentions into words, both Lana and Ronald found they had a better chance of having their needs met, and neither felt abandoned by or intruded upon by the other.

Will Letting Out My Anger Make Things Worse?

Although Roz and Terry had been married for eighteen years, their relationship had never been fulfilling for either of them. Their interests were different. He was always pushing her for more time and attention; she needed a lot of time to herself. He liked to see a lot of people each weekend; she liked to read and tidy the house. They both had full-time jobs that required overtime, and they learned to keep away from each other. She was disappointed but did not want to leave Terry; she was finally getting the quiet she needed. He wanted more closeness, connection, and warmth, but he was not ready to leave either. With other people, Terry knew how to talk about himself, his feelings, and his desires, but with Roz, he was silent.

Terry gained in confidence, did well at work, and developed new friendships. He had a few brief affairs when he was out of town, which occupied his mind more than he would have liked. Terry talked to Roz about going to therapy together, but she refused. She was afraid; she did not want to hear all the ways she had failed him. Roz did not understand that a therapist would not be opening a door for Terry to vent his rage but would find ways for each of them to hear the other's story. They could share their needs, fears, and sadness, and the therapist would not take sides. Roz's unwillingness to go to therapy was further proof for Terry that she was not willing to change or meet his needs. She withdrew further.

After several months, Terry recognized that divorce was the only answer for him. He told Roz late one night, after the children were asleep, that he wanted to end the marriage. He had dreaded the moment and did not know what to expect. Roz was quiet and un-responsive. Was she in a state of shock? Did she not care? Did she know and expect this? Terry had no idea what was going on inside her, and he did not ask.

Roz was shocked and furious. She was afraid her rage would drive Terry away. She felt suspended in time, speechless. She did not know how to protect herself. She thought only that if she sat perfectly still, he could come back more easily. In the end, Terry and Roz never really talked about what had brought Terry to the point of divorce. Roz withdrew even more and depended on her job and her children to fill her life. Terry went on to create the life he wanted with another woman.

If Terry and Roz had met with a therapist to learn to open to each other, they might have found their way to love again. Roz's inability to express herself and Terry's unwillingness to initiate her into the language of intimacy denied them a life together. Instead they offered each other silence. Roz was left with a residue of bitterness and rage that she felt for years.

How Can I End This Fight?

The joy and connection that can arise in a committed relationship of two people who love each other—who know each other well; who know how to let go of some things and work out others; who try to be generous of spirit, slow to anger, eager to please, and ready to make amends—is a lifetime project.

When Jay first married Esther, he did not want to sound like his parents, bickering over every little thing and then saying how much they loved each other. For several years, he did more agreeing than he normally would have in order to keep the peace. However, as he matured he was no longer willing to swallow his disagreement, or his feelings of hurt and anger. He needed to work out ways of disagreeing that were not a fruitless back and forth, yet that allowed him to speak.

Jay found that some strategies made things worse:

- Leaving the room.
- Swearing.
- Denigrating the other person's position.
- Saying "You never" and "You always."
- Refusing to talk.

Slowly Jay and Esther began to discover possible ways of moving forward:

- Asking where, when, and how to have a conversation: phone, e-mail, appointment, at home or office, morning or evening?
- Planning what would work for each of them as the opening step of a conversation.
- Allowing five minutes for each partner to state his or her position, with no interruptions, in as neutral a way as possible.
- Listening fully and quietly to each other.
- Working out a compromise: your way this time, my way next time.
- Finding again that old feeling of love or cooperation and choosing to act from that place.
- Deciding to be happy rather than right.
- Letting go of what was most divisive, knowing each partner has been heard.
- Learning the joy of saying, "Yes, dear."
- Making a joke.
- Saying "I know that is important to you, but it really does not work for me."

Using these techniques, Jay and Esther were able to find areas of agreement. To begin the process, you might try starting with statements like these:

- I want to express my needs in a way that you can hear them.
- How can I do this better?
- I would like to tell you when I am closing down.
- Will you let me know when you are starting to close down?
- I want this to be a useful conversation.

Why Is It So Hard to Say I'm Sorry?

Kenneth had trouble saying, "I'm sorry." And he had more trouble promptly accepting an apology when it was offered. In therapy I taught Kenneth and his wife Janice something valuable I had learned at a couples retreat. To reject an offer of peace is worse than whatever affront has occurred. When Janice said to Kenneth, "I'm sorry I lost your favorite CD, I know it bugs you when I don't put your things back," he stomped off and said, "It's too late for apologies." He made a bigger mistake than Janice did by losing track of the CD. Instead, if Kenneth had said, "I am angry *and* I accept your apology," he would have moved toward ending the confrontation.

Besides saying "I'm sorry," here are other words that can de-escalate a confrontation:

* I wish this were over.
* I miss you when we fight.
* I am sorry I did what I did (or said what I said).
* I did not mean to say it that way.
* I want to stop talking to you this way.
* I thank you so much for apologizing.
* I thank you so much for helping me stop this downward spiral.
* I thank you so much for being able to laugh when I need you to laugh.
* I need you to warm my feet, even if you are furious.
* I need you to kiss my neck—right here—and then you can be angry again.
* I love you underneath being furious.
* If I say I was wrong, will you say you were wrong?

These are some of the statements you might use to end a fight and reconnect. Discovering when and how to refine the words for your situation is part of the creative process of living in a loving relationship. Using these phrases early and often can protect you from later blowing up and blowing apart.

Why Is It So Hard to Say Yes?

Saying "yes" does not come easily. For some people, saying "no" does not come easily either. Learning how to say both "yes" and "no" is a necessary component of a working relationship.

Justin felt he was giving up his own sense of direction—indeed, his very identity—when he simply said "yes." To protect himself Justin never agreed to Janet's first suggestions, even on such simple things as which restaurant to go to for dinner. Janet was amused at first by his contrariness, but as the months went by, she found herself annoyed. He would ask her where she wanted to go for dinner, and anything she suggested, he would negate, even if he had said the choice was up to her.

One day Janet asked Justin if he would try to speak the words of agreement and see what that was like for him. As he examined himself, he found that he was worried he would be controlled by Janet and become passive like his father. He realized that learning to use *both* words—saying "yes" when he could and "no" only when he truly disagreed—seemed like a good idea. He learned to ask Janet for her opinion and then give it serious consideration. Over time and with consciousness, and with Janet praising Justin when he did say "yes," Justin learned to overcome his negativity.

How Can I Say No and Not Hurt Him?

For Claudine, as for many women, saying "no" was difficult. She feared that by disagreeing, or negating what was going on with a "no," she would alienate Paul, and he would blow up. She pondered how to say "no" in a clear, undemanding way that did not injure their ease with each other. She chose a good person to do this with, as Paul was a reflective, thoughtful man who wanted explicitly to work on their relationship.

In the face of a disagreement, Claudine first had to recognize the value of her position. She then needed to say "yes" to herself for having that position and wanting to maintain it. She had to recognize her desires and what was in her best interest, and she had to support herself. When she needed to say "no" to Paul, she finally learned to tell him, "No, I cannot do that because it does not work well for me. I want to preserve our loving relationship. I want to work out a solution that suits both of us."

Claudine had to learn that saying "no" does not mean "I get my way" or "I don't care about you." It just means "No. Now let us negotiate." She came to feel less threatening if she prefaced a "no" with an affirmation of their relationship and a willingness to hear Paul's side of the equation. If she then followed with a negative, she restated her affection for him, offering her idea of a solution and asking for his.

Conclusion

Living in partnership is far more than the comfort of companionship. A committed relationship offers a place to love and be loved, a place of centering and grounding. At its best, people are able to grow and love in the security of acceptance by another. But relationships are not easy. To keep love alive, to keep respect and acceptance operating, takes consciousness and kindness.

CHAPTER 3

Accepting Differences between Partners

When we meet new people and begin to know each other, we look for similarities. Any differences may appear as charming eccentricities. Sometimes the differences are even the attraction. When living together, though, the differences become less charming, more annoying, and the areas that rub. And new differences will surface later in a relationship, when both the known and the unknown differences may cause difficulty. While people may fall in love with each other because of (or in spite of) differences in race, religion, or nationality, after commitment the differences in sense of time, use of space, use of money, amount of sexual desire, entertainment preferences, communication skills, and emotional intelligence can create problems.

When the river has branches and partners choose different courses, therein lie moments of conflict. In this chapter I address the dilemma of how to move in the same general direction as your partner when you are drawn toward different tributaries on the river.

Don't You Have Any Feelings?

Hilda and Larry had been married for eleven years when Larry's mother died. Hilda wanted to know what he was feeling about his mother's death. He felt he had said all that needed to be said. Indeed, he felt rather lucky that his mother had lived so long and that they had developed an easy, loving relationship. Hilda felt she was being left out of his inner workings, so she pushed and probed. Larry told her that she seemed to want him to be sad, miserable, and grieving but that he just wasn't. He did not think he was being dishonest, nor did he think he was in denial. He felt that he should be able to grieve in his own way. He was relieved at how easy letting go of his mother had been. He occasionally missed her and on odd occasions found himself talking to her in his head, but other than that, he hoped he could live his life as well as she had: being optimistic, loving, connected, and satisfied. Was that not enough?

Hilda did not feel this was the whole story for Larry. In a period of self-exploration, she was learning to recognize, name, and own her own feelings. She was excited by the dimensions of herself that were unfolding. She wanted Larry to be exploring himself too. One evening, after they had turned off the TV, Hilda started to talk to Larry about her feeling that they were not being open with each other. "We each need to be able to mourn and grieve, talk about hard times, and connect intimately," said Hilda.

Larry felt that her expectations were preventing her from hearing his actual feelings, but he did not confront her directly. While he sat with her and appeared to listen, he actually tuned her out. He felt misunderstood and did not want to try again to clear up the misunderstanding. He just kept his temper under control and hoped Hilda would give up. Larry was not interested in analyzing his feelings at this time, and was uncomfortable with Hilda's probing of herself and of him.

Hilda told Larry that she felt *she* was doing all the grieving. She was trying to listen to his pain and grief, but nothing was coming from Larry. She told him she felt this was unfair. Larry began to think about what he might be feeling. He knew what he was thinking. Although he was afraid he would create a fight, he decided to tell her what he was thinking: "I don't like this conversation. I am feeling pushed by these demands. I need to mourn in my own way. My way is different from your way, and I want you to accept my way. I said good-bye to mother before she died and I feel a quiet calmness about her death."

All of these statements were about Larry, by Larry, so Hilda could not contradict him. This was his truth. He could not be wrong about his own feelings. In his statements, Larry did not blame. He didn't say, "You are pushing me." He said, "I am feeling pushed by *these* [not *your*] demands," allowing Hilda to recognize that she needed let go of the demands and find other ways of talking to Larry. By expressing himself this way, Larry gave Hilda room to change her position and save face. She could then say:

- You are right.
- You don't have to mourn my way.
- I will try to accept that you are doing what is best for you.
- I realize I don't verbalize my feelings the way you do.
- I am aware that I often disagree with you just to disagree.
- I know I have been pushy lately.

After this conversation, Hilda was able to respect and accept Larry's different way of handling his feelings. She could begin to enjoy Larry's company instead of trying to make him be just like her.

Differences occur in many areas in a marriage, and learning to accept the other person the way he or she really is can be major effort. The desire to be with someone who is the same is not confined to Larry and Hilda. Money, time, emotion, and love are only some of the areas where differences arise that need to be explored with love, curiosity, and respect.

Why Are You Always Late?

Liz and Bill were planning a trip to Paris to celebrate their twenty-fifth wedding anniversary. They had dance and concert tickets, friends to see, and a few business appointments. Their main issue was time. At home Bill felt he was always waiting for Liz, while she felt he was always early. He would stand at the front door ready to leave; she would rush up a few minutes late and then run back to their room for whatever she had forgotten. She wanted to leave later than Bill; he wanted to be early. Liz did not even wear a watch. Time became a sore spot between them.

Not wanting their old argument to be part of the Parisian experience, Bill asked Liz to talk to him about their differences in this area so he would not feel he was waiting for her all week. She agreed. They learned a lot about each other in this exchange. Liz told Bill that she did not like to hurry. She felt agitated when she hurried. She felt that she was *not* always late, just leisurely. She felt pressured by Bill always wanting to be early. On the other hand, Bill felt anxious as time was passing. He feared being late and making others wait. That was his underlying mindset.

Now knowing clearly how each approached time, they felt more accepting of each other's way, but they still needed to reach a new arrangement to be comfortable in Paris. They talked about how to handle the vacation, exploring the issue without blame. They decided together that during their vacation Bill would not be the person responsible for time, for getting them to where they were to go, or for generally moving the show along. That was to be Liz's job.

Their first day in Paris Liz accepted Bill's offer to loan her his watch, and she took charge of the schedule. They set off for a day of sightseeing, followed by dinner and a dance performance in the evening. Liz never asked Bill what time it was, and they were delighted with how easy their change of roles had been. During the entire week, they were never late for anything. On returning home they found, without planning it, that Liz was getting ready a little earlier and Bill was getting ready a little later, and they began meeting at the front door, both ready to go out. Neither one felt pushed or rejected.

Getting stuck in old behavior and allowing the irritation to go on and on is often part of a long-term relationship. Bill and Liz's creative solution, to see their part in the dance and then change that part, brought joy and tenderness into their daily operations. Just talking about their different styles and the underlying mechanism that kept them entrenched gave them a feeling of ease, about the subject of time and about the two of them together in the world.

How Can We Find Our Way Back to Intimacy?

Before marriage, Laurie and Peter were very open and intimate with each other. They examined and analyzed everything they said to each other, turning over the inner meaning of each exchange. They kept a running dialogue on whether or not they were well suited for each other, and in what ways. They liked to talk about how to live together in a fair and equitable way that allowed each of them enough space, yet not so much that they grew away from each other. They wanted to grow together, to change in similar ways, and to explore the world internally and externally as partners. They discussed how they would treat their children and what other people were doing with their children—both the styles they admired and the behavior they promised to avoid.

For Laurie and Peter, life was not lived if not analyzed. Then they married. After marriage, all the intimate conversations stopped. They were loving with each other. They were still compatible and companionable. But they stopped talking about their inner lives. Then Laurie told Peter that she missed their previous conversations.

The inner exploratory talk aroused love in her. Where had he gone? She wanted back that intense, dating time, but she could not find a way to engage Peter.

As for Peter, he was glad that all that talk was over and he could get on with his work. He was tired of Laurie pushing him to connect at what he felt was a juvenile level. Laurie was so full of words. Where was the softness he remembered? How could he get her off this broken record?

I met Laurie and Peter when they came to me for marital counseling and began to talk about their two very different ways of being close. I asked them to politely express their needs without being demanding, so the other could hear without turning away. Laurie spoke of the value she placed on openness, self-exploration, and listening. To her, that was the essential element in being a couple. She missed hearing about Peter's thoughts and feelings, and she missed telling him about herself. Peter said that sharing personal thoughts and feelings had been a great way to get to know Laurie and to figure out whether they were suited for each other, but now that they were married, he was no longer interested in this kind of self-disclosure.

After noting this major difference and speaking about it, they had to decide if their relationship was worth working on, whether compromise could leave them with enough of what each wanted, and whether they could rekindle their passion, which had been eroded by this difference. As they talked, the marriage contract shifted. During the counseling sessions, Peter began answering Laurie with the fullness she wanted. Afterward they would go out together, staying out until ten or eleven o'clock, not talking about the children but about themselves, as I had suggested, and then going home and climbing naked into bed, where the talk continued.

Peter began to remember the interest he previously had about the inner workings of people. He realized he had been closing off part of his experience, and how closed he had become to Laurie. He experienced again the pay-off of openness. His renewed sense of connection with her—of feeling with her and for her, of finding he *did* know the language of emotions—led him to be willing to be intimate with her when he had something to say. At first holding back was hard for Laurie. She had a self-righteous fervor in her desire to reclaim Peter. She felt she was the deep one, that he had let her down, but she also began to appreciate that the time off from personal excavation could be light and fun. Letting go of their traditional stances did not come easily or quickly but grew out of their affection for each other and for the value of staying married. Laurie let up on pushing Peter to talk. She realized that their relationship could have different modes and that having fun together could be intimate too.

If Only We Had Been Candid
About Our Differences

Frederick and Sabina met at college. They were both members of a left-leaning political group that was opposed to war and the use of nuclear power for military purposes, and in favor of taking action to protect civil liberties. They shared these values, loved their fellow activists, and talked long into the night about the world they wanted for themselves and their children. But Frederick was loath to talk about his family, and for a time this made Sabina hesitant about getting involved with him.

Sabina had grown up in Fresno, California. Her parents, both schoolteachers, had been socialists in the thirties. Sabina knew Frederick had gone to a prep school and that his liberal politics had grown out of his elite background. Sabina knew little about his family except that Frederick was one of five children who all talked to each other on the phone every week.

After two and half years of dating, Frederick and Sabina went to New York to meet his family. Frederick seemed uptight on the flight, but Sabina attributed this to the life-determining decisions they were now facing at the end of their senior year. What next? They had talked about joining Teach America, but had not yet made the necessary calls. As they flew over Philadelphia, Frederick, trying to appear offhand, told Sabina that his family had money and lived quite well. He told her she should not be shocked when they arrived at his parents' apartment. The enormous apartment, he had neglected to tell her, was on the two top floors of a hotel overlooking the East River, with internal stairs, a suite for the maid, and a four-sided view of Central Park and the city. Decorating the walls and tables were magnificent paintings and art objects.

Sabina had never imagined anything like this. Frederick seemed slightly ashamed and did not want to discuss the scene, though they usually talked about everything. Not wanting to be loved for his money nor abandoned because of his social class, he had played it safe and said nothing until the very last minute. Polite and reserved, Sabina hid her amazement and her dismay, which was what Frederick seemed to want from her. She liked the generous hospitality of Frederick's parents and their easy acceptance of her. They liked her straightforward intelligence and warmth.

In the back of her mind, Sabina wondered how she was going to tell *her* parents about this development. Would they hold wealth against Frederick's family? Her parents professed to be open to all people of any race or creed, based on who they were and not what they were, but did this extend to the wealthy? And how would Frederick's parents react to the small, middle-class home in central California where she had grown up? These were big questions. Sabina ended up picking up Frederick's unease about this aspect of his life. She never again talked to Frederick about their different economic backgrounds.

Sabina and Frederick married and raised children, but they kept having the same fight. Frederick's way of keeping difficult subjects from her until the last minute and then expecting her to take in the surprises and not react to them was difficult for her. She liked to be included in his thinking, planning, and knowing. When he kept her in the dark until he was forced to tell her something, she felt belittled. She worried that he was afraid of her reactions or, worse, not interested in her opinions. The early exchange on the airplane had been a forerunner of what was to come.

Only after many years did Frederick learn to say to Sabina: "I am having trouble telling you this, but you need to know. I have waited too long to tell you this. I hope you will accept my apology. I don't know where this will end, but this is what I am facing right now. I want you to think well of me, so it is hard to tell you." And Sabina learned to say: "I want to know what you are thinking. I want to know the difficult things that arise for you at work and at home. I want to share the good times *and* the bad times with you. I can handle whatever you tell me. Nothing is so bad that I don't want to hear about it. I know your way is to avoid talking about difficult subjects, but you have to know leaving me out is destructive."

Through this kind of exchange—using phrases that had to be repeated over and over—Sabina and Frederick were able to change their way of talking with each other.

Why Can't We Ever Do What I Want?

The recreational time of Michelle and Gordon was thrown off by Michelle's travel for work. When she was home, she needed down time, and Gordon, having been alone all week, needed Michelle to come out and play. Each an only child, they had little experience working out the daily ins and outs of two people sharing space and time. Gordon soon found living alone during the work week easier than arguing with Michelle about what they were going to do during their free time. He began to dread the weekends when Michelle only wanted to stay home. Michelle began to feel that the demand to perform at home was too similar to the demand to perform at work. She felt she needed to re-evaluate who she was and what she wanted to do. She realized she had little energy left for being in a relationship.

Michelle and Gordon needed to talk. The basic question they asked each other was "Do we want to stay together?" They both said yes. Then they asked each other: "How can we work this out so the time we spend together is easy and pleasant? Do you think we need someone to help us, perhaps a therapist or a mediator?"

Both Michelle and Gordon were reluctant to get involved with a professional. They were trying to save money, and they did not want to spend the time they had together in an office. They decided to ask Gordon's brother and sister-in-law to talk with them somewhat formally, three times, away from the children. Everyone thought this would be a great idea. Gordon's brother Bob and his wife had noticed the pulls and pushes between Gordon and Michelle. Having other people listen to them helped Gordon and Michelle speak with less insistence and less self-righteousness, and they also found it easier to listen to each other.

Bob and his wife suggested a compromise, but Gordon and Michelle ultimately found their own solution. If Gordon would allow Michelle to relax at home on Friday night and Sunday night, then she would be happy to go out with Gordon and do things from Saturday morning through Sunday afternoon. Michelle was not sure this would be enough quiet time for her, but she was willing to go along with this compromise for one month and then meet again with Gordon, Bob, and his wife. They met as a foursome for this purpose four times in all, until Gordon and Michelle had a flexible weekend schedule that accommodated both their needs. With outside help they were able to negotiate a compromise that honored both of them.

How Can I Compromise When I Am So Afraid?

When living in a partnership, each person can find it difficult to lightly hold onto his or her desires. Compromise, which too often can feel like losing, is also a way to achieve peace. Doug and Betty needed to learn to compromise. Their power struggle had immobilized them, destroying their intimacy and their respect for each other.

Married in midlife, both Doug and Betty were deeply independent, and both were aware of their core self and of their individual needs. They started out enjoying each other's strength and purposive approach to life. Doug was especially delighted with Betty's self-sufficiency because his first wife was helpless, dependent, and depressed. But after Doug retired early, he wanted to travel and even expressed the desire to move away from where they had lived for eighteen years. Betty firmly said she did not want to change her life. She was younger than Doug and did not want to stop working. She told Doug she was afraid that if she took several months off to travel, when she returned she would have no clients and no income. She did not want to be dependent on Doug's retirement income, waiting for him to dole out money. Nor did Betty share his desire to move. Doug's plan was not right for her.

The struggle escalated. "I want it my way," they both said, each trying to make a case for his or her position. To follow was to give in, to be weak, to be dependent. Neither one was ready to say, "Yes, I want to do this with you, your way." Betty found it hard to compromise. All her life she had seen her mother give in to her father, becoming—in Betty's eyes—a dishrag, a follow-along, a second-class person. Betty did not want to be like her mother. Any time she reluctantly agreed with one of Doug's suggestions, she felt smaller than before.

During the weeks I worked with Doug and Betty, they began to recognize that their deepest wish was to be together, in harmony, and that to do so would require compromise. The only way to stay together was to find a solution that suited each of them. They needed me, as a neutral third party, to hear what they were saying to each other. As a therapist I could help them see the fears that led to the stalemate. Slowly Betty realized she would have to meet Doug halfway.

Letting go of her need to produce money full time was difficult for Betty. Her self-sufficiency arose from staying on the path she knew. Change was frightening. More than just changing her mind, travel meant constant change—hotel rooms, cars, bathrooms, and restaurants. She was embarrassed by her fear of different places. Moving to a new city involved all these issues on an even more demanding level. She wished she could embrace variety, but that was very difficult for her. In our therapy sessions, Betty got in touch with her fear of change and was finally able to say, out loud, "I have never told you this, and I blush as I say it. I don't want you to think less of me, but I am dreadfully fearful of change."

Hearing Betty's underlying fear made Doug more understanding of her reluctance. He realized her fear of change stood in her way, not the money issue or her desire to block him. Feeling compassion for Betty, Doug grew to realize how much his need to be the leader in the relationship was interfering with his ability to respond lovingly to Betty. He told her this.

Having spoken her fear out loud, Betty was able to contemplate letting go of the vigor of her resistance and think about how she might try traveling with Doug. She imagined that traveling as a couple might be much more pleasant than when she had traveled alone. Having spoken his need out loud, Doug was able to loosen his grip on the leadership role. However, he continued to find it difficult to give up his stance as the victim whose needs were never met. While appreciating Betty's effort to move toward him, he was careful not to push her too fast, nor to denigrate her for her fear, realizing that only with time would he really believe that Betty meant what she said. Betty finally agreed to travel with Doug twice a year for two weeks at a time. While accepting Betty's offer to try traveling as a first step toward change, Doug offered to drop the idea of moving. Affection and mutual respect slowly returned.

After this first successful mutual decision, Doug and Betty learned to laugh about how difficult compromise can be. They teased each other, "Who is going to say 'yes' first today? Is it my turn or your turn?" They gave each other "frequent flyer miles" for being willing to compromise. And Betty ended up loving the experience of traveling with Doug, which was nothing like the disruptive, anxious time she had imagined. By truly listening to each other and being willing to try out new behavior, they no longer felt torn apart.

Speaking internal feelings aloud and then learning that feelings can change allows us to soften our long-held beliefs and cooperate with each other. Every power struggle in a relationship has underlying motivations and feelings, and when conscious conversation takes place, compromise is possible.

How Are We Going to Live Together After All These Years Apart?

Carl believed that marriage was like a trap or a prison. When he met Dora at a friend's house during a visit to New York, he did not imagine that he could create a life with this lovely, brilliant woman. He had been through an unhappy marriage and he dreaded entering into another relationship. He feared that he would again feel trapped by the togetherness, leave, and break someone else's heart, as well as his own.

Then Carl and Dora began to call each other and to arrange occasional cross-country trips. Carl lived in San Diego, where he had a good job at a hospital. Dora worked for an advertising agency in New York City. Three years into their transcontinental love affair, Carl began to entertain thoughts of marriage. He felt more complete with Dora in his life, more serious about commitment, and also protective of the relationship he and Dora had built. Dora felt the same way, so they decided to marry. They also decided their marriage would not be traditional; they would still live separately. This would *not* be an open marriage; they just wanted to continue as they had but with a formal commitment to each other.

In the past both Dora and Carl had been in relationships that included shouting matches and verbal abuse. They wanted to avoid that behavior. They each understood how quickly their own anger could flare up. They had worked hard to keep the peace they had achieved. Because of their long phone conversations, they did not feel superficial with one other. When Dora was with Carl, she felt a deep sense of connection, beyond words and personality. She felt that this was the person she wanted to have know her fully in this lifetime. No one else had ever been this close to her. For the first time, she felt safe in being known. She appreciated the acceptance she felt from Carl, for herself just as she was.

Before saying their vows, Dora and Carl discussed their answers to these questions:

- Why do we want to live separately?
- How often do we want to see each other?
- What expectations of loyalty do we have?
- What does an unconventional marriage mean to each of us?

Dora and Carl agreed that either of them could bring up the subject of living together at any time. If one of them wanted to try living together, he or she should not be afraid to say so. Having reached agreement and pleasure in their decision, they celebrated their marriage. No surprises. This would be a nontraditional relationship, and nothing would be taken for granted.

After their wedding, Dora and Carl continued living on opposite sides of the country. Their encounters were gracious and flowing. Each was entirely willing to do what the other wanted because they could do as they liked when they were apart. In fact, they were afraid of losing their rapport if they were together too long. They continued to have their most intimate conversations on the phone. They were open about their insecurities, irrational thoughts, pleasures, and achievements. More than ever before in their lives, they could talk about anything. But in person, they found it hard to dip into those waters. Instead they made lots of plans to be out of the house, walking and shopping in the city or seeing friends. They liked to show off each other. They liked to come home and talk about the people they had met that evening.

A few years later Dora checked in with Carl to be sure he was still comfortable with their arrangement. She had been concerned at first that her friends and family would not understand her lifestyle, but found herself to be very comfortable. She loved her time with Carl and she loved her time alone. She would not have wanted either to be full time. Carl agreed. Their arrangement of living apart while being married was working for him as well.

All of a sudden Carl's hospital was merging with a national medical service and he was offered a position in the city where Dora lived. Before making a decision, they both laid out their concerns and expectations. They approached the ultimate conversation with love and expectations that they could work it out.

Dora began: "I want to be sure I still have time to see my friends without you coming along, and I want to have some time to myself. I am sure we can arrange that. I hope you will bring some of your furniture and works of art to my place; I will put some of my things in storage. "

Carl spoke about his needs. "I am concerned that I don't know many people in New York City. I am afraid that I will be experienced by you as a situation that requires work, as someone who is a burden. I don't know what my new life will be like. I want your help."

Each spoke of the joy of being together. Dora said that she would be delighted to have him with her, that when she arranged her weekends he would be there. Carl spoke of his anticipated joy of waking with her each day and of sleeping together each night. They also agreed that they wanted to be able to go to bed and get up in the morning when each wanted to, without having to comply with the wishes of the other.

Being in a long-term, committed relationship and living apart has become a viable choice for a growing number of people, a choice that allows a couple to be together in a way that is comfortable for both. Some couples have two houses, which they keep and use, alone or together. Others spend summers and travel time together, living separately during work time. To sustain both the non-traditional lifestyle and the intimacy of marriage, ongoing conversations about how the situation suits each person are particularly important.

Why Can't He Treat the Children the Way I Do?

The most challenging issues in a relationship often arise around parenting. Each of us brings to parenting different experiences from our childhood—approaches we believe are valuable as well as those we want to avoid. Parents hold a great deal of attachment to getting it right, knowing the answers, doing it my way, and being unwilling to compromise. How can I comprise when the welfare of an innocent child is involved? Yet couples often have different views on discipline, allowances, eating practices, chores, schedules, and behavior.

How should toilet training be accomplished? Should we spank our children when they misbehave? Should our children go to private school or public school? Can the children have dessert if they don't eat their dinner? How much freedom should they have, and at what age? Can our daughter go to a rock concert on a school night? Can our kids and their teenage friends be allowed to smoke marijuana in the basement? Can our son's girlfriend sleep in his room? Should our children choose their own college or their own spouse?

Sometimes the differences in child-rearing techniques are minimal for one partner and huge for the other. Each topic requires conscious conversation. Even if one spouse leaves child-rearing decisions up to the other, sooner or later a different point of view will need to be addressed. The parent who is uncomfortable with what is going on needs to raise the subject calmly, candidly, and with hope of a resolution.

Wally always praised Alma's way of caring for their children. He felt that she had received good parenting while his own had been negative and harsh. He wanted Alma to treat the children much as he imagined her mother had treated her. Alma was a calm gentle presence. Perhaps tending toward the lenient, she set limits for the children in a deep quiet voice. But Wally often came home from work tired and disgruntled, while the children—wound up and hungry, waiting for dinner—would get noisy. When Wally would shout at them, "Settle down, you kids," Alma would shiver. The children are so small, she thought, and he is so big. Does he realize how gruff and mean he sounds? If she were to say something to him, might he retaliate? Because she felt correcting Wally in front of the children would be wrong, she ended up protecting her husband, not her children. By so doing, she also protected herself. The children learned to avoid Wally in the evenings. They made up games without him.

Alma finally overcame her fear of Wally's temper and chose a time when the children were not present to intervene. She said to him:

- I want this conversation to go well. I want to speak to you from my heart.
- I want you to hear me out and think about what I am saying.
- Sometimes when you are feeling stressed, I hear you address the children sharply.
- I want the children to know your loving, easy side. I don't want them to be afraid of you.
- I don't want to be afraid to talk to you about things you do that bother me.
- I want you to listen to me.
- I need to protect the children, and I need you to help me do so.
- How might I help you with this?
- Thanks for listening.

Wally listened to Alma in silence. He later thought about what she had said, and decided to attempt to be more pleasant with Alma and the children. He was not always successful, but he learned to apologize when he found himself yelling or barked out sharp commands. His modified behavior and his ability to apologize made a huge difference to the family, while also teaching the children to resolve their differences without yelling and to be able to say "I'm sorry" when appropriate.

Conclusion

We love each other's differences *and* we are annoyed by each other's differences. At times we wish for a clone as a partner, someone who agrees with me about everything, someone to whom I don't need to explain myself, justify myself, defend my position. But then we realize how dull that would be. We go back to the business of discussing, listening, compromising, and finally accepting what is not going to change.

Acceptance is important when couples are faced with differences that are disruptive. Some of our partner's behavior isn't going to change. One way to coexist is to recognize that whenever something is bothersome to one person that seems to be unchangeable to the other, the bothered person needs to consider accepting what is. Peace sometimes meaning letting go of wanting change.

CHAPTER 4

Bringing Words of Love to Intimate Moments

Speaking aloud the words of love, appreciation, and sexual arousal does not always come naturally. Some people choke up when trying to speak about their love. One partner may have to take the lead, accepting the other's hesitancy while allowing extra time to find the heartfelt words of love, desire, and appreciation that will enhance the intimacy. All the examples in this chapter offer words, but many people rely on silence, touch, looks, and mutual understanding. For those who *want* conversation during these personal moments, the examples here will help you find your words.

How Can I Learn to Say "I Love You"?

Anita loved Joseph but she had a great deal of difficulty squeezing out words of love and appreciation. Joseph told Anita with glowing, positive words how he felt about her—that he admired her cooking, her clothes, her comments, her way of being—but she was unable to return his words of love. She knew he wanted to hear the words, but she was afraid her words would not please him.

Joseph began to ask Anita to say nice things to him. He encouraged her by suggesting she start small, with what pleased her at that moment, and build up to maybe one day saying "I love you." He told her that sometimes he wondered if she really did love him.

Anita reminded him of all the ways she showed her love. Was that not enough? Because Joseph persisted, she agreed to begin in small ways:

- I like your tie. I like all your ties.
- Thanks for helping with dinner.
- Thanks for helping me find my words.

Anita soon realized that if the comments were small, she did not feel like she was saying them to make Joseph compliment her. To hear herself saying nice things made her realize how foreign these words were for her. She thought of herself as generous and open-hearted, and she did not want to appear coldhearted. When Anita realized that compliments could be given with no implied demand, she felt freer to be generous in her expressions of pleasure toward Joseph. After a few months, Anita was ready to go further:

- I like going out with you.
- I like your friends.
- I like the way you treat me.
- I like your skin, your hair, your body, even your knees.
- I like to make love with you.
- I love you.

Finally the words "I love you" came out of her mouth. At the same time Anita could hear her father's voice: "Don't tell people that you love them. They will take advantage of you." But she was *not* her father, and speaking the words of love to Joseph felt good.

Even when one person does not have some sort of mental block that prevents the expression of appreciation, a couple may choose not to speak lovingly to each other. But to keep a loving relationship alive, words that describe the good feelings need to be spoken out loud. Praising each other for the cooperation, appreciating growth that has occurred, giving thanks for the effort that went into change—these words nourished their relationship and increased its value in the heart of each partner. At different times each of them was able to say:

- I like your easy laughter.
- I love your ability to let go of anger.
- I am touched by your willingness to accept me just as I am.

Instead of taking each other for granted, every couple can learn to acknowledge a helpful, kind, touching, beautiful act, and comment on it with pleasure. An exercise to help couples get in touch with what they love about each other asks each person to make a list of the partner's attributes that are pleasing, and the lists can be shared out loud.

How Can We Keep Love Alive?

Some couples knew the words of love during their courtship but stopped saying them as the years passed. The words may have been lost from disuse. To return to the expressions of love may take a good-faith effort to use the sincere words and behavior that reflect what you initially loved about your partner. You might begin by asking each other these questions:

- What did we like to do together when we first met?
- What were the words you liked to hear when we first met?
- What were the words you liked to say when we first met?
- What did we talk about?
- Which friends did you feel comfortable with? Which friends did you enjoy spending time with?
- How did we used to treat each other that was special and unusual?

Compliments that include superlatives—you are the best, the most, the greatest—are appropriate for expressing your delight. To succeed, you need to pay attention to both your partner *and* your innermost feelings. Notice when you have a good feeling and then express it. When both partners are able to simultaneously do this, the results are immediate. If only one partner has the self-awareness to try, change can still happen.

Offering small, precise compliments can make a difference:

- Nice dinner.
- Nice hairdo.
- Glad you had a nice day.
- I appreciate that you have started to ...
- I want to be with you tonight.
- I am glad you are my spouse.

When we want love from the other, we first need to freely give. When we initially offer compliments and kindness, we may be rejected, batted away as too foreign, insincere, or untrustworthy. But if we stay with our new behavior long enough, our partner will begin to change. In the meantime, the one who has undertaken to sincerely speak words of love will simply feel better, even if the other does not respond. Compliments and words of love need to be freely given; only then might something come back.

How Can I Talk about What Works for Me in Bed?

For most people looking into a partner's eyes during the act of making love creates a stronger bond than any other form of connection. To enter the body of another, to have another person inside—this can be the ultimate loving union of body, mind, and spirit. For some couples, their physical merging becomes the ultimate connection with the universe. However, without the words and deeds of closeness and love, sex can be a cold, purely physical activity that creates a sense of alienation more than a connection. Words of desire are part of lovemaking. The words spoken before, during, and after making love are often recalled more vividly than the physical act. These words are remembered and caressed by the mind, replayed, explored, and analyzed far beyond the awareness of the lover. But without similarly intense feelings being expressed on both sides, sex is not enough to bind a couple together for a lifetime.

To reach a point of agreement on whether or not to make love sometimes requires a conversation. Even if one person clearly does not want to engage, both partners need to express their desire (or lack thereof) and feel they have been heard. Even if neither partner feels desire, stating the obvious and talking about the reasons behind this momentary lack of desire can lead to a loving connection.

Loni did not feel like making love as often as Stan, but she did not like to say no to him. She also did not like pushing herself to please him. Loni knew Stan was tired of asking and being rebuffed. She began to fear Stan's approach and Stan began to fear the inevitable rejection, yet he kept approaching and she often said no. They had never worked out a way of clearly expressing their feelings without hurting one another.

Loni finally asked Stan if they could choose a good time to talk about their different sexual needs. She told him she wanted the conversation to be different from their usual ask-and-be-rebuffed talks. This gave Stan time to think about what he wanted to say, how he wanted to say it, and when he would be ready to talk—not in the middle of a difficult driving maneuver, not just before work, not when he was tired. He decided that Saturday morning suited him, so he asked Loni, as considerately as she had asked him, if Saturday morning would be good for her. They decided to sit side by side, not wanting to risk their looking at each other turn into glowering. They decided to give each other three minutes to talk, with no interruptions and no defenses, just an exploration of how each felt, what each felt was possible, and what they hoped for most. And if all went well, they might even talk about how to get both their needs met, but that might take another conversation.

By the time Saturday morning arrived, they were making comments about how this conversation was the sexiest thing they had done in weeks, making jokes about what to wear, whether Stan should shave, whether Loni should put on lipstick and perfume, whether touching would be okay. Just having established that they both wanted to talk calmly about the situation helped them become more relaxed.

Loni wanted Stan to begin, but telling him to talk first sounded too controlling to her, so instead she said to him, "I want you to go first. Will you?" And he was willing. They laid out the plan: Each was to speak about what he or she wanted and hoped for, rather than what the other had been doing wrong.

Stan talked about wanting to express his love through physical contact. He said he would be willing to ask less often if he were met with interest more often. He confessed that he really did not know when to ask or how; he felt quite at sea about reading the signs. He even admitted that sometimes he initiated sex when he did not want it, just to make Loni feel bad.

Loni listened carefully, relieved that she could find some place of agreement with Stan and that she was not poised to rebuff. She said feeling desire was difficult when he was always so ready. She wanted him to be a little hard to get, and sometimes she wanted to initiate sex.

After both had spoken, they agreed on a three-minute silence. The silence gave them time to pause, relax, and be open to each other with a clear mind, less antagonism, and less of an agenda. They wanted to truly hear each other.

Stan was not sure about waiting for Loni to initiate lovemaking. He was afraid nothing might ever happen. Since he was ready most of the time, he did not like the idea of repressing his natural instincts, but he was not ready to say this to Loni. Instead, once they began talking he asked, "How often do you want me to ask?"

"Once a week," she answered.

Stan asked how he would know when she might be interested. She told him she would be clear through her words, by the way she undressed or by the way she would begin to stroke him. She said she might ask him to make love more than once a week because having some control over the exchange would make her feel sexy.

Stan was still not sure if this would work for him, but said he was willing to try. Loni was not sure either, but she also was willing to try. They both realized they still might create impediments to connecting and would need to check in with each other from time to time. Loni gave a lot of thought to how she could hold Stan in her mind and heart throughout the day so she might be interested in making love at night. Stan realized he loved the sexual act but that perhaps his need for Loni to satisfy him had more to do with himself than with Loni, and he guessed that she sensed this. He, too, decided to focus his thoughts more on what he loved about Loni and all the different physical and verbal ways he could express his love to her.

What Do People Say While Making Love?

Some people prefer silence while making love, perhaps with just the sounds of *ooh* and *aah*. Others like to talk. Either way is fine as long as both parties are in agreement. After their conversation about sex, Loni and Stan began to talk more during lovemaking, sharing the fantasies they had created about each other throughout the day. They began to create joint fantasies and verbally enhance them for several nights. They were playful, open, and arousing. Sometimes they described what they were feeling physically, what their point of pleasure was in the moment, what felt especially good. They began to tell each other what they wanted, and asking what the other would like and whether it was feeling good.

Their lovemaking was not a steady upward spiral. From time to time, Loni and Stan needed to go back to their side-by-side conversation, renewing and sometimes refining their intentions. They discovered that the first conversation had paved the way and that the subsequent talks were easier. Over the years, they continued to talk about the words and gestures of their love, and about the different ways of touching and appreciating that turned on each of them. Stan was surprised that Loni liked to be told how good she felt to his touch. Loni was interested to learn that Stan responded positively to her compliments on his appearance and the way he dressed. They would never have learned these things—and enhanced their love—if they had not dared to begin that first conversation.

How Can We Keep Sex Exciting?

Jon and Andrea married when they were young. They felt as though they personally had discovered sex and were better at it than anyone ever in all of history. They made love often and easily. Years passed. Health issues interfered; sleepiness interfered. They were happy to cuddle, slow to arouse.

Suddenly Jon and Andrea decided they needed to jump-start their love life. They went to a sex-and-spirit workshop. They practiced simultaneous breathing. They read high-class literary pornography; they looked at saucy pictures. They read about the G-spot and about prostate stimulation. They went to a shop with accoutrements for sexual stimulation, including videos, CDs, books, and paraphernalia for men and women. After buying a few small items, they went home, lit some candles, got out the lubricant, and began to pleasure each other. Lighthearted but not silly, delighted and pleased, they enjoyed the new titillation and varieties of stimulation that were available to them. Their daytime love merged into their evening lovemaking.

More important was the conversation. These are the sorts of things Jon and Andrea talked about over the next few months:

• What qualities attract you to people you pass on the street?
• What qualities attract you to people you meet at a party?
• What do you find attractive when you talk to strangers?
• Which gestures or body movements do you find attractive?

After describing the attributes they each find stimulating, they went on to talk about their own lovemaking. Over a period of a few months, they began to say things like:

• What do you like me to do to you as we begin to move toward lovemaking?
• What do you especially like that I already do?
• What do you think you might like me to try?
• Where would you like to make love?
• Do you like to make love on a schedule or by surprise?
• Who do you like to have initiate the act?
• Do you want me to move differently?
• What forms of foreplay do you like?
• What is one thing I do that does not work very well for you?
• Do you like me to talk or to make sounds without words?

Stating their wishes and having them met was arousing, which was what Jon and Andrea wanted. They engaged in sexy talk while in bed and sometimes on the phone. They talked about what they were going to do with each other the next time they were in bed together. They sent sexy e-mails to each other. They made love more often and looked forward to it with anticipation.

To keep love alive and passion sparking, a couple might talk about their fantasies:

- Who do you want me to pretend to be tonight?
- What do you want me to be wearing?
- Who else shall we pretend is in the room?
- Where shall we pretend we are making love? Indoors or out? In which country? In which city? On a boat? In an airplane?
- Do you want me to tie you up with silken scarves? Pretend or real?
- In fantasy, who do you want to have sex with for your birthday?
- How many people would you like to make love with at a time?

Jon and Andrea loved their shared fantasies, but for some couples this could be dangerous territory that needs to be approached with caution.

How Can I Talk about My Sexual Attractions?

Couples with a long history of openness and acceptance may step gingerly into conversations that other less-secure couples would never enter. Talking about outside attractions is a high-risk activity to be tried only after both partners agree that it is exciting. To open the subject might sound like this:

- Do you want to hear about the people I meet from time to time for whom I have a blip of attraction?
- I will tell you about my outside attractions only if you are okay with it.

- Are you interested in telling me about your attractions?

Taking time to ensure the primacy of the committed relationship, the conversation might continue:

- I have been feeling attracted to a person in my office. He has nothing on you.
- I feel so alive sexually these days that I can't help but notice the sexual energy of other people. Is this true for you?
- I am not going to act on this. I just want to talk about it so it is not secret.
- My relationship with you is absolutely primary, even off the scale of any other connection, but I do feel attracted to a few other people in my life.
- I don't want you to feel threatened. If you do, I don't have to talk about this. If you can handle it, I would like to hear about your experiences with other people and then we would have yet another way of knowing each other.

How couples handle these conversations is unique to each. The subject needs to be acceptable to both partners. Some people prefer their spouse's sexual needs be met outside the marriage. Some couples like to talk about their extramarital thoughts and even their affairs; others never want to hear a single word about a partner's outside attractions. The conversations are unusual and often charged. If only one partner wants to share his or her thoughts and feelings on this subject, then the conversation should not be pursued. Starting slowly with reassurances and simple fantasies, while revealing only a little at a time, may help relax the other partner. Checking in on how the information is being received can prevent hurt feelings. Sex is a sensitive area and calls for curiosity, tact, and nonjudgmental listening. For some couples, discussing outside sexual attraction is too high risk to even consider. Others may find it arousing.

Can I Be Intimate without Sex?

Couple-hood takes many forms. Some attachments are mostly physical while others have no physical intimacy. Some relationships are built on companionship, shared interests, children, professional interests, or convenience, along with a lack of sexual desire. The degree of physical intimacy need not be a given, but can be discussed and agreed upon. Some people meet and agree from the beginning that physical intimacy will not be part of their relationship. Others try lovemaking only to decide that their intense friendship is better than the momentary passions of the body. They may like cuddling, holding, and touching; they may not. I have seen many variations around this issue. As long as both partners agree, their relationship works. But agreement takes conversation; it cannot be assumed.

Although Joe and Zandra live together and love each other, they do not make love. They have been a couple for fifteen years; they are each other's best friend. They have seen lust and passion ruin other relationships, they know how desire and longing negatively affected their lives in the past, and they do not want to tempt fate by entering those waters with each other. The initial conversation between them was entered cautiously and in a somewhat convoluted manner. While they were dating, neither made any attempt to touch or kiss the other. Finally, Joe felt he had to say something. He told Zandra that while he liked her a great deal, he was not interested in physical contact with her or anyone else. He asked her if that was all right with her. She told him she felt relieved to hear his attitude toward sex. She, too, did not experience lust and desire as other people seemed to.

Over the years, the couple reviewed the terms of their relationship from time to time. Their conversations included the following questions:

 • Is it still okay with you that we don't touch or hug?

- What if I change my mind in a few years? I may need to raise the subject again.
- Do you talk about our arrangement with your friends?
- When the whole world seems so sex driven, do you feel strange that you are not?
- Do you refrain from sex to please me?
- Do you ever wonder what physical desire would feel like?
- Have you ever had a sexual encounter? What was it like?
- Is our arrangement still okay with you?

The wild, unbridled urge to bring their bodies together does not exist in this relationship. But Joe describes their relationship as open, spacious, intense, close, intimate, and fulfilling. For Joe and Zandra, the verbal intimacy is more important than sex, and they want their friendship to last.

Conclusion

Many different avenues lead to an intimate relationship. Finding ways to meet each other with an open mind and an open heart, receiving and giving the best of ourselves to our loved one, and accepting what our partner gives of his or her inner self allows us to live in the fullness of our love. Letting go of the record keeping—who did what to whom, who gave more—nourishes the bond that is the foundation of a loving relationship. Realizing that our love is more valuable than our sense of discomfort releases us to unite in acceptance. Peace and harmony arise. The love radiating out provides positive energy to the whole relationship and to those around us.

CHAPTER 5

Speaking Candidly during a Major Life Crisis

Ideally, during a major life crisis we want someone with us, someone who can help paddle us to smooth waters. But the ideal is not always so easy. The needs of each partner may not match. The responses of one partner may not work for the other. In this chapter I will describe how people in relationship deal with four types of adversity: illness, substance abuse, job loss, and infidelity.

Illness

When a serious illness is discovered in one member of a family, all members are affected. Some are comfortable with the change in needs and caretaking; others are not. The capacity of a family to respond to an illness varies widely, depending on the duration of the relationship, whether children are still at home, and the needs of aging parents. When ill, we all want someone we love with us during appointments and treatments, someone we love in the house to bring us what we need, but often this is not possible. Talking about the expectations, the needs, and the reality is a necessary step in keeping all family members aware of what they can give, what they ask for, what to appreciate, and when to say thanks. Awareness of others and acceptance of each other's limitations will lead to the growth that can come from a crisis.

How Can I Talk to Him about His Prostate Cancer?

Carlos and Marisa were married for only two years before Carlos was diagnosed with prostate cancer. Both were in their forties, both had been married before, neither had children. They had been thrilled to meet someone with whom they were so compatible. They both loved to travel, snorkel, scuba dive, river raft, and ski. They planned weekend trips away from their home in Seattle. Their rhythms and excitement were a good fit, and they were happier than they had ever been. They felt as though they were destined to be together for a lifetime.

Shortly before their second anniversary, Carlos noticed that he was urinating more frequently, and often with pain. He was also beginning to find his job as a newspaper editor difficult because he was physically inactive all day. Tests and more tests began for Carlos. Carlos and Marisa did not talk about their fears—cancer and death—before they knew what was wrong. Ultimately, though, Carlos's doctor told them the diagnosis: "Carlos, I am sorry to have to tell you that you have prostate cancer." Carlos and Marisa were stunned. Each for the sake of the other had tried to appear stalwart and unruffled. After the appointment they spoke only about how open and clear the doctor had been, how they would trust him to take care of Carlos.

Inside Marisa was disturbed and frightened. This was her new, young, lusty husband, and suddenly she was faced with an illness she knew nothing about. She did not want to burden Carlos with her feelings. She wanted to be available in whatever way he needed. They talked about the medical and physical aspects of the cancer, but neither broached the emotional effects—the feeling of loss, the anxiety about the changes Carlos might undergo, and the fear about the unknown future.

Marisa and Carlos spoke of their love as they had before, continuing to focus on the wonder of their meeting rather than their fear that their sex lives might be drastically changed or that their time together might be cut short. Marisa was deeply afraid that Carlos would die. She felt alone but did not want to burden Carlos with her emotions. Carlos did not seem to have any fear. In the silence that grew between them, Marisa felt that Carlos was abandoning her just when she had become comfortable with being in a close, communicative partnership. They were kind and polite with each other, but the cancer was eating a hole in their intimacy.

Instead of talking about illness, fear, and loss, they made plans for trips and celebrations. They spent their time together talking about travel, not cancer. They did not talk about the fact that the cancer had gone into the lymph system. They treated the situation as a straight line: surgery, radiation, recovery, and then back to life as it was before. But after the surgery, which went well, their life was different. As the periods of silence became longer and more frequent, Marisa felt a growing hole in a marriage that had held so much promise. She began to despair of ever reconnecting with Carlos.

One night, as they were going to bed, she spoke out. She told him she needed to hear how he was feeling about his body, his cancer, his new physical changes, and their life together. She wanted to know the rational and irrational thoughts he had. She wanted to be right there with him. Carlos responded by saying he wanted to know what she was feeling as well. They were both in this, and she needed to be open too. He did not want to be protected by her. He missed their closeness. He did not want his cancer to be the main thing going on in their lives. He acknowledged that this illness was huge for him, and he told Marisa he needed to know what his illness meant to her.

Marisa said she was afraid for Carlos's life and sad about all he had to go through. She feared he would die and she would be alone—that the dreams they had of growing old together were not going to come true. She felt the operation and subsequent urinary and erectile difficulties had aged him. As she said these words out loud, she began to have a feeling of relief. Carlos was listening to her again; she was able to talk to him.

Carlos wanted to ask Marisa more about her feelings:

- How much do you love me? Can you still love me?
- How do you feel about finding new ways to be physically loving?
- What are your thoughts about my dying too soon?

Marisa did not want to burden Carlos with all her concerns, so she had already thought about the questions she wanted to ask:

- How do you feel about your changed body?
- How do you feel about dying?
- How can I be more supportive of you?
- What do you fear?

As he began to talk, Carlos realized how much he had been holding back: "I am afraid of the frequent PSA tests," he told Marisa. "I am afraid of the return of cancer. I hate the idea of dying soon and leaving you. I fear that you will reject me because I may never again have ordinary intercourse. I wonder what your reaction is to some of the drugs and external devices that could to help us in bed."

Marisa said she was interested in knowing what was available and figuring out which method of enhancement would suit them best. They were talking. She said that loving, cuddling, kissing, and physical contact felt good to her. They were talking a lot. The relationship was in a new place of openness and trust. And their willingness to talk about their feelings had brought them back to their intimacy.

How Can I Tell Him I Can't Meet All His Needs?

Cally and Mike had been married for twenty-nine years when he had a heart attack. They were both frightened by the event. Not yet sixty and with their children grown, they were looking forward to many years of travel and pleasure. They clung to each other in the first weeks after the heart attack, speaking of their love and interdependence in new ways and feeling the intensity of their need for each other. They were both more expressive than they had been in years.

The image of living the rest of her life alone filled Cally with fear. She did not want to be alone; she wanted Mike by her side. They stopped taking each other for granted and began to celebrate every little movement toward health. They called their children more often; they expressed their appreciation for their friends. Each day they were together, even while visiting in the hospital, they considered a wonderful gift. Cally often read to Mike from funny books people had sent, and they laughed and laughed over the same things.

When Mike was finally released from the hospital and returned home, he was instructed to take it easy for two months. Two exercise sessions a day along with some stretching and walking were prescribed. He did not go to work. Cally stayed with him. She learned how to cook the Dean Ornish diet for Mike. She moved their bedroom into the room on the main floor that had been her office. They had a bathtub with a Jacuzzi put into the downstairs bathroom. The first week home was a kind of vacation. They rented videos and watched them at odd hours. They worked on the picture albums that had not been brought up to date for three years. Friends came over to check on Mike. Cards, letters, and phone calls flowed in.

While Cally was fine physically, as the second and third week passed she began to feel imprisoned in a house that no longer felt like her home. When the phone rang, someone invariably wanted to speak with Mike. She was not seeing her friends, she did not have a project apart from caring for Mike, and she felt frustrated. But Mike seemed happy. Cally felt that if she complained or drew his attention to how trapped and bored she was feeling, he would be hurt, and maybe react with anger or sarcasm. She did not know what to do. How could she begin a conversation with Mike that would not result in her accusations and his withdrawal?

As time went on, Cally began having fantasies of divorce:

- As soon as he is well, I am leaving.
- Now that I know what he is really like, I can't stay with him.
- He is rude and jumpy.
- He is anxious about his health and takes it out on me.
- Is this how I am going to spend the rest of my life?
- Is this the person with whom I want to spend the rest of my life?
- I never wanted to be a caregiver.
- I don't feel good about myself as a caregiver.
- This is unbearable.

When Cally found herself spending half of every day in a rage, she decided to seek help. As her therapist, I encouraged her to vent her rage in my office, not at home, which she did for several sessions. She also began to call her women friends and plan activities outside of her home. She complained about Mike to her friends, who mostly felt she belonged with him and just needed time to find her way back.

Cally continued to keep her rage from Mike, who was still home taking it easy, reading his magazines, and shouting to her whenever he needed anything from the kitchen. One night Cally's control broke down after he again complained about the repetitiousness of grilled fish and leafy greens. She shouted at him, reminding him *he* was the one who needed this food, *her* cholesterol was fine. If he was not happy with her meals, she said, then he could do the shopping and the cooking. And she told him she was unhappy, she was thinking of leaving, and she definitely could not go on like this. She hated being trapped in the house with him just sitting around. If he was going to be home all day, he needed to do something more than be an invalid.

Mike was stunned. He went to the bathroom. Cally sat at the kitchen table, deflated and silent, shocked at what she had done. She did not know where to go from here. She had never thought she would expose all of her rage to Mike. Cally panicked. She should not have been so blunt. Maybe she didn't really want to leave and be alone. She called out to Mike: "We were talking in here. Isn't illness a time for change? What about my needs? Don't they matter?"

Mike came back looking rather shaken. She began to ask him all the questions she had not dared to ask:

- How do you feel now about your health?
- How do you feel about being home and not productive?
- How do you feel about having me take care of you?
- How do you feel about my feelings?

They talked about the phases of their marriage, the roles and responsibilities they had each taken on, the unhappiness, the distance, the repetition. They cried together because they had hurt each other so much. Mike asked Cally not to leave. She said she was not at all ready to leave, that she had frightened herself by saying so. She needed him to be kind to her. He needed her to be kind to him. He talked about how frightened he was to do anything that might bring on another heart attack. The next one would be worse and more likely to cause death. The first had occurred on an ordinary day, doing ordinary things—standing around in the office talking to a few people. The next heart attack could come anytime. He was not at all ready to die. He felt he was in the middle of his life. He wanted Cally with him. He did not want to be alone, not for one night. He needed her very much.

Mike told Cally he wished they could be as loving as they had been when he was in the hospital. He said he was upset at being so helpless. She said she wanted gratitude and recognition, that she had needs too. He said he was ready to try to be more independent, picking up groceries sometimes and going out to restaurants again. She told him having his help would mean a lot to her.

Cally appreciated Mike's willingness to engage in the conversation. She recognized that she had stopped talking about her feelings, as had he. She wanted to be sure they would be open with each other at this level more often. She and Mike developed a theory that intimacy is a muscle, like the heart, that needs to be used well, cared for, and exercised. Unused, intimacy can shut down. Overused, the relationship can burn up.

Cally had not said anything cruel during her outburst. Instead, the conversation renewed their relationship. She was glad she had started the conversation. When one person begins to talk about their feelings, the other person usually finds a way to join in. Some conversations are better than others. Mike and Cally merely needed a little practice revealing their less friendly feelings in ways that were not sharp or cruel.

Substance Abuse

The use of addictive substances can create massive impediments to the flow of love in a relationship. Couples and families can be seriously damaged, sometimes permanently, by addictive behavior. To get to the other side of addiction with an intact relationship takes clarity of boundaries, a limit on acceptance, and love.

What Can I Do to Protect Myself from His Drinking?

John had several drinks every night on the way home from work. By the time he got home, he was drunk and often fell asleep on the couch. Stella predictably got angry. The more Stella hated John's drinking, the more she yelled at him about it, and the more defensive John became, the more the couple fought. That was their stuck place for years. While talking with her therapist, Stella realized she needed to find a way out of her part in the destructive pattern of communication. She needed to loosen up about John's drinking in ways that would force him to take responsibility for himself. And if he did not become more responsible, she realized she needed to consider leaving the relationship.

Stella began to look at the triggers that aroused her anger, and figure out ways to avoid them. She had been making a lovely dinner every night that was ruined by the time John finally came home. Self-righteous for doing her duty, Stella would eat too much, get furious with John, and stop talking to him. And he, of course, would stop talking to her when she was in that mood. Stella finally began to think about what she needed to let go of so she would not feel self-righteous and angry. She told John she would no longer cook dinner for him. She also told him she would not be home on Tuesday and Thursday evenings until ten o'clock. She told this to John quietly and clearly, not saying anything about his late nights or his drinking.

At first, John did not pay attention to her. When he finally noticed that Stella was not always around, he was stunned. He yelled at her. "Why aren't you here any more? Where is my dinner?" She stood her ground. She quietly and firmly restated her intentions, this time adding her discontent in terms of her own needs, not John's failures: "I cannot wait for you night after night. I don't like your drinking. I now have interests of my own. I am going to be out Tuesday and Thursday evenings. I want to go out to dinner with you one night a week, before you have a drink. I love you. I am concerned about you. I am not leaving. I am going to take better care of myself."

John seemed to listen this time. Stella felt gratified that she had stated her case so calmly. After a while John began coming home a little earlier on Monday, Wednesday, and Friday. He began to ask her about her evenings out. Although he was not yet able to slow down on the after-work drinking, he did acknowledge the problem. For Stella, this was a major step. She continued to let up on pressuring John. Change slowly entered the marriage. After a year of the new arrangement, they began making plans to take their first vacation in years.

Addiction to alcohol as well as addiction to work or volunteer commitments can pull one spouse away when the other wants togetherness. Living with addiction is particularly hard for the non-addict spouse, who must realize that changing the behavior of the addict is impossible. Stella wanted change but could only take charge of her own life. John began to notice something different was happening in the house. When Stella stated her own position quietly and calmly, John was able to listen and decide what he wanted to do. He began to go to Alcoholics Anonymous meetings and to meet with Stella's therapist.

Why Doesn't My Husband Care That I Drink?

Vivian drank only in the late afternoon. The long, dark winter afternoons got her down. She had no kids, no job, and no fun. Her husband, Eliot, worked late, did not expect dinner, and when Vivian began drinking enough for him to notice, he stayed away even more. He had closed his heart to Vivian years earlier, and while he had no plans to leave her, he gave the relationship no attention. Both of them stored up their grievances, withdrew into silence, and kept away from each other to avoid an explosion. Vivian wanted

Eliot to treat her as he had years ago. Eliot wanted to come home to the happy, engaged woman Vivian used to be. Neither was ready to speak about their needs.

What could Vivian and Eliot say to each other to overcome their impasse? Eliot might start with verbalizing what he wants:

- I want you to stop drinking.
- I want back the girl I married.
- I will try to be pleasant to you.

Vivian might reply:

- I want you the way you used to be.
- I want you to want to come home.
- I would stop drinking if I believed we could have something together.

On hearing just a small statement that Eliot wanted her, Vivian might consider sobriety. On hearing that Vivian would stop drinking and be present for him, Eliot might feel for the first time in years a stirring of compassion for her. He might realize that he missed his wife and that he too felt lonely. He might come home for dinner and talk to her. Tentatively reaching out, speaking short brief statements of interest in improving the relationship would give Eliot and Vivian the possibility of reconciliation that will not arise in silence.

Job Loss

Like a tree branch across the river of life, job loss can cause serious disruption to a couple, even to a whole family. To hang onto the tree, to leave the river, to find a new river, to do whatever is called for takes flexibility, clarity of mind, and a foundation of values.

How Do I Respond to You Losing Your Job?

Caleb had been the family's main bread winner. Tania only worked part time as a substitute teacher. She mostly took care of the children and the household. The computer company that employed Caleb suddenly closed down just as their first child started private school and their toddler was enrolled in a private nursery school. Neither Tania nor Caleb had ever lived in a home where someone lost a job. They were not prepared for this crisis. Already overwhelmed with the expenses and time demands of rearing two children, they both found themselves angry and blaming. Short-tempered with each other, not wanting to give up their lifestyle, they had very few outlets for their frustration and no solutions.

Caleb's company paid for employment counseling and placement, but many others were also seeking his kind of job. He was not yet willing to take any job. Tania asked for more time as a substitute teacher, and Caleb agreed to drop off and pick up the children according to their school schedules. Both Tania and Caleb were frightened. They stopped talking to each other. They each hoped the other would rescue them from this situation. They went about their daily tasks, with Tania resenting Caleb for not doing more of the housework and grocery shopping. He was afraid to do so, lest that become his life. Because they did not say these things to each other, resentment festered. They had both been taught to keep their emotions to themselves. When failing at that, they acted out, rather than talking about their underlying feelings: failure, fear of being stuck in the house, wanting to be rescued, wanting life to be as it had been. They were afraid to tell the other members of their family what was happening. They grew more and more isolated. Caleb became depressed. Tania developed stomach pains.

How were Caleb and Tania to discuss their fears and frustrations with each other? They might start by saying:

- I'm sorry this is happening to us.
- I am frightened that this is going to go on forever.
- I am on your side. We need to work together on this.
- I need your help at home when you aren't working. As soon as you work, I will take over again.
- I need you to support me, not go silent.
- We have more time to be together as a family. Let's make plans.

With these simple expressions of what is going on for each of them, not blaming, not turning the fear into silence, Caleb and Tania might be able to work together work toward solutions to their problem. The first step entails a change in their way of relating.

How Can I Help My Partner with His Professional Difficulty?

Life can bring us into situations we never dreamed we'd have to face. A man is surprised to learn that his partner has been behaving illegally and has to spend time in jail. A woman is squeezed out of her business with allegations of wrongdoing by her partners. People can be sued, or sue a customer, and spend time and money tied up in the court system. How is a spouse to behave in these situations?

Situations like this often bring couples closer together in the fight against a common enemy. Listening, agreeing, assisting in planning, and loving may come more easily than before the crisis. But what if a man believes his partner was in the wrong and was rightfully convicted of a crime? What if a woman believes her partner was rightfully sued. Do you stay or leave? Whom do you talk to? What can you do to protect yourself? Dealing with this kind of crisis is much easier when one partner agrees with and supports the other. But when confronted with an act that is morally repugnant, what is a partner to do?

The best course of action is not easy to find. Some spouses stay, some leave. Do you leave for murder but not for a lesser offense like fraud? Those who leave do so slowly and only after considering the children, the ties of love, and the bond of commitment. How does the wrongdoer handle his or her misstep? What is the degree of remorse? Supporting a person who acknowledges guilt and feels remorse is easier than supporting one who denies any wrongdoing and defends himself in the face of incontrovertible evidence.

The conversations that take place are as important as the final decision about the relationship. The quality of the connection that arises around the lapse in judgment or self-control often determines the response. Here are some questions that need to be asked:

- What was your part in this?
- What do you plan to do?
- How did this happen?
- When you don't talk to me about this, I find it hard to support you.
- Help me to understand.
- How would you like me to support you?
- What would you do if you were in my place?

Haste and reactivity may not bring you to a place of fairness. Answers need to be pondered, perhaps while looking deeply into the heart. With understanding will come the decision to be supportive, to be angry, or even to end the relationship. Perhaps the response will ultimately be "I can't live with this" or "I cannot be a part of this." A partner's role is to determine if his or her love can survive this event. The law will administer justice.

Infidelity

When we enter into a marriage or commitment contract before God, family, and friends, we are agreeing to a monogamous relationship, unless otherwise stated from the start. The long-term relationship, in which each person is fully committed to the other, is a cornerstone of our culture and of most religions. The immeasurable joy of growing old together without jealousy and the threat of outside sexual liaisons creates a container for love and security. Yet people do sometimes wander, look outside the committed relationship, meet someone else—and one partner or the other ends the commitment, sometimes abruptly and with no conversation. People do have love affairs even when they have promised fidelity. Sexual attraction is a potent force. Although infidelity—a breach in the marriage contract—should not to be taken lightly, an affair does not necessarily have to lead to divorce.

Some people may enter an affair as a way to end a marriage. For others, the affair has nothing to do with the marriage. Many times the faithful partner does not "hear" that the wandering spouse wants to keep the marriage going. What comes through is only the rejection, the lies, the attraction to another, and the initial response is to want to end the marriage. Pride and the desire for punishment and revenge get in the way of making a reasoned decision. What matters is that the conversation, once the affair has been revealed, will determine whether the couple wants to stay together, whether they both feel they can restore trust, and whether they value what they have built together as a couple.

Do I Have to End the Marriage?

"I will never trust him again," Becky told me. "Trust him about what?" I asked. "Coming home on time? Being sweet, kind, and helpful? Being a good father? Being a good provider? Being faithful? He *is* trustworthy in every area except one." Yes, being faithful is important, and Becky could not get beyond the lack of trust that was a result of Sid's affair. No matter what Sid said, Becky felt she could never have him near her again. After learning about the affair, Becky tried to continue living with him. Three months later, she told him she could not go on with the marriage and she was going to a lawyer. Their marriage did not have to end like this. Why would Becky throw out everything good because he put his body next to someone else's? Clearly a lot of conscious conversation was needed to get this relationship back on track.

If a marriage is to survive infidelity, conversation needs to follow the discovery or revelation of unfaithfulness. Becky might have begun talking to Sid like this:

- I am furious, hurt, sad, and disillusioned.
- I wanted a real, monogamous marriage with you.
- I wanted you to love only me.
- What was going on with you that made you do this?
- What did you think I would do or say?
- Did you feel you were risking our marriage?
- What in you gave rise to this need?
- What in our marriage would you want to change?
- What will happen if I insist that you never do this again?

Sid's answers to these questions could help Becky understand him better and see ways they might work together to stay married. Sid did not want Becky to leave. He loved her, the children, and their life together. He was sorry he had hurt Becky. He had not taken into account her reaction to his affair. After responding to Becky's questions, Sid might have said:

- All the love you have felt coming from me all these years is real. I do love you, completely.
- I have not lied about my love for you, ever.
- This act had nothing to do with the love I feel for you.
- I did not do this to hurt you.
- I am so sorry I have hurt you.
- I hope you can forgive me and continue to love me.

Becky may have been moved by Sid's avowal of love and his wish to stay with her. She may have found her heart responding to him.

Conversations like this do not often take place over such a heated issue. By offering these words as a way of entering such a conversation, my hope is to help couples move away from blame and punishment and toward loving discourse. Too often in our culture, an act of adultery means a divorce must follow. This should not be a given. Sometimes a relationship is worth saving.

How Can I Tell Him I Am Seeing Someone Else?

Ida had tried for eight years to get Ivan to respond to her needs, but she felt she was getting nowhere with him. To everything she wanted, his response was "not yet," "we'll see," or no answer. He was away for long periods of time for work. He wanted a very simple, quiet life. She wanted to move into Boston; he wanted to stay in Roxbury. She thought he needed a better job; he thought she should be earning more. Theirs was a difficult match.

Ida began going out with her own friends on weekends and leaving Ivan home. Then she found out about Internet dating and starting spending time on the dating Web sites. She was fascinated to learn all about other men without ever meeting them. With fantasies of finding Mr. Right, she joined one of the dating services. By paying a small amount of money and answering a series of questions about her interests, her personality, her job, and her family, she could read all about the men who were listed. She looked at men's pictures and read their answers to survey questions: Are you married? Are you happily married? Do you want to date? Do you want to fall in love? She worked out of her home office, so most days she had hours alone to secretly be on the Web.

Trying on fantasy people was a lot of fun. Ida began to correspond with a very promising man who wanted to meet her. He lived nearby. She knew she could easily meet him for coffee when Ivan was out of town. She did not meet him, but she was hooked on the fantasy life. She went to the Web site a few times a day looking for other interesting men. Ida did not tell Ivan about her secret fantasy life. She knew he would be furious. A small, muscular man, Ivan had a fiery temper when pushed too far. But she did tell him that she did not like the way they were together and that she wanted more from him.

Many months went by before Ida talked to me, her therapist, about her online searches. I thought Ivan would be angry about her deception and her fantasy life. I encouraged Ida to begin to introduce Ivan to her interest in seeing other people. Perhaps this would give him a chance to be more responsive to her. I suggested she tell him she wanted a more active social life, that she wanted to go out on dates with him outside the house. Ida decided to tell him that she had fantasies about dating, that she wanted them to go out on dates as a couple, and if he was not interested in spending time with her, she would see friends, including men, without him. I encouraged Ida to move the conversation toward telling him that she was already trying online dating, felt guilty, and intended to stop. I felt that she needed to open an opportunity for Ivan to hear her need and then to develop a social life with her. I warned her that he might become very angry and that would be his right. She could not legislate his feelings. She needed to begin telling him the truth so she would not be burdened with guilt for her betrayal. She was frightened of telling him the truth. She needed to find her words.

Ida finally said to Ivan: "I know you will be angry. I would be too, in your place. But I hope you will try to stay calm and hear me out. I need you to know the truth about me and what I am doing. I have been communicating with men through a dating service on the Internet. I don't want to do this anymore. I want to go out with you. I want us to have friends who are couples. I want our lives to include more special time with each other. I am sorry. I hope you can forgive me and move forward with me."

Ivan was angry with Ida; he did yell at her, and then he stalked off. She sat quietly and waited. She again apologized, speaking to him in a kind voice. After several days he was ready to sit with her, to find out what she wanted from him, and to discuss how they were to go forward with their marriage. He questioned her from time to time about where she had been and where she was going. Ida liked his being aware of her even as she sensed his underlying fear. She responded openly and truthfully, and she no longer went online for socializing with men. Ivan went out on dates with Ida as long as Ida did the planning. This worked well for both of them. Ivan continued to carry some distrust, but with time this was dissipating.

Can We Renegotiate the Conditions of Our Marriage?

When they marry most couples expect to have a monogamous relationship. The few people who are able to keep their marriage alive while including outsiders hold each other as primary in both word and deed. They make each other feel that while they may view others with lust and interest, the primary loved one is far above and separate from everyone else.

Every five years or so, couples may chose to talk about the expectations they each have about monogamy, or about the openness of their relationship. As people change, their needs, interests, and feelings about the marriage may change. If the lines of communication are kept open, the marriage has a better chance of surviving and thriving. At some point, both partners may want to change the rules. They may find rewriting the rules together to be fun. With openness and humor, the subject can be discussed, tamed, and diminished in intensity. The conversation is so intimate that it might move the couple toward a deeper connection and replace the titillation they may have been seeking outside their marriage.

Conclusion

Difficulties arise in life beyond the expected. Each couple deals with a crisis in its own way. Suffering and challenge, endured together, can bring people closer. Sometimes how a couple handles the difficulty makes it clear that these two people do not belong together. However, conversing with care and attention needs to come first. Abrupt decisions and actions without forethought may permanently damage one partner and bring guilt to the other, leading to the end of a relationship that might have been preserved. With time and conversation, a couple can weigh all the aspects of the relationship that are working well against the reason for and the pain caused by the infidelity, then come to a decision about preserving or ending the relationship.

CHAPTER 6

Making Divorce Less Disruptive and Painful

Couples tend to seek a divorce when disagreement drags on for days, weeks, months, and years; when fighting, yelling, distance, rudeness, and blame are commonplace; when one person does all the apologizing; when one person is always right; when one person is always angry; when one person lies; when either or both are abusive or violent; when respect, love, and kindness disappear for long periods of time. Endless periods of silence or emotional distance bring partners to the point of breaking up. The chaos, trauma, violence, and disruption that come with divorce can seldom be avoided. When partners who were once in love, attached, and committed to each other seek a divorce, their feelings too often turn into anger, hatred, and revenge.

Although great pain is inherent in the situation, severing the committed connection does not have to be destructive. People who are operating from a conscious place can stop to review the strengths and weaknesses of their partnership. They can consciously choose what they want to achieve, what they want to say, and when to speak. They can use words that are not violent and blaming, words that are not destructive of the other's self-esteem, words that do not permanently wound. Parting does not have to arouse feelings of shame and a sense of failure. When two people come to a point where they believe they have given the relationship their best, they have explored all ways of working together, and there are no more ways to try to stay together, then the words, "no more" must be spoken. The goal can be to preserve a modicum of friendship so the partners do not destroy each other and, when they have children, so they can continue to function together as parents.

With quiet but clear statements, perhaps some of the pain can be averted. A conversation might sound like this.

- I loved you once. I do not anymore. I cannot go on living with you. I am sorry it has come to this.
- I am sad that our hopes and plans for a lifetime will not be fulfilled.
- I want to do this in a way that preserves enough respect for each other that we can make a decent arrangement for our divorce.
- I know I have not been easy to live with. I want to stop living together.
- I want to be able to meet you in the future without acrimony.
- I want to continue to parent our children with you as well as possible.
- I respect you as a person but find I cannot live with you.

Some people leave without ever understanding what was preventing an easy, intimate relationship. Others, with the help of a therapist or a mediator, choose to explore what went wrong. Some of these couples, once they get out of their habitual adversarial positions, find a new ease in each other's company, hear each other in new ways and sometimes even decide to stay together. I know of painful, damaging divorces, and I know of quiet ones as well. I believe two people can find their way out of a partnership with decency and even with compassion for themselves and their partner.

I Can't Remember Why I Married This Person

At the suggestion of a therapist, two people who were threatening to divorce wrote down all the things they were attracted to in the beginning, and all the things they had enjoyed and learned from their relationship. They each agreed to include this list in a letter to the other. They also agreed not to critique what was written, and to trade lists without comment. This exercise can bring some couples back together. For those who proceed with divorce, the letter can remind them that the whole marriage was not bad, that they were not failures. The letters can be retained and reread over the years.

To remember the good times, a person might write one of these statements about an estranged partner:

- I was drawn to you the first time I met you by your ...
- I love your laugh.
- I enjoyed talking to you about politics
- I liked going to the beach with you.
- I loved you the night we cried and held each other after the cat ran away.
- I like the way you cared for me when my mother was sick.
- I admire your ability to listen to my office talk.
- I learned from you to be more patient.
- I learned from you how to sail a boat.
- I will always remember the time you ...

These are hard words to find and hard to say out loud during the difficult periods of the marriage. I believe people can find the words to express the pleasure they once had in a partnership, the reasons for wanting to leave, and their hopes for the future apart, even as they are leaving.

What Am I Going to Say to End This Marriage?

Finding the words that will allow for a break without severe personal damage takes forethought, the intention not to harm, a conscious choice of words and tone, and finding the appropriate time and place for a conversation. When hope of reconciliation is slight, statements like the following might be appropriate:

- This marriage is not working for me.
- My part in our alienation is that I can't let go of wanting you to be different in these ways ...
- I realize I should accept you as you are, but I am not able to do that.
- I want to leave this marriage. I feel that my part in the breakup is my desire [my fear, my need, my habit], which is different from yours and does not work with your desire [your fear, your need, your habit].
- Please let us do this with care.
- You are a fine person. You are a lovable person, but not for me anymore. I cannot go on living with you.
- We both know what has happened between us. I hope you don't feel like a failure at marriage. I am trying not to feel like a failure. We both have learned a lot about what sort of person we would like to be with. Let us seek mediation, split up our possessions, and go our own ways.

What Will It Take to Forgive?

Years after a divorce, many former partners find their way back to civility, some even to forgiveness. With time and reflection, some are able to understand their role in the break up. Some even rediscover a fondness for a former partner, including an ability to integrate her into family occasions. By softening to the other, by accepting a former partner for who he is, by accepting his presence in the life of their adult children and grandchildren, a way is found for forgiveness of one's self and of the other.

Here are some possible words that can lead to forgiveness:

- Only after several years was I able to recognize my part in our break up. I now see what I did that got in the way of our getting along. I am sorry for that and I ask your forgiveness.
- I realize the ways I withheld my love. Please forgive me.
- I realize how judgmental I was and I am sorry.
- I realize I did not keep my word. I have deep regrets about that.
- I realize how little I did for our togetherness. I am sorry about that.
- I realize how dependent I was and how that must have felt for you.
- I know I have made life difficult for you by not fulfilling the terms of our legal agreement.

This kind of apology will go a long way toward lessening the tension between former partners, thereby allowing them to be together for family events and to be civil to one another.

How Will We Tell Our Parents?

"Soon after we decided to end the marriage, we needed to tell our parents. I found that very difficult. I put it off for days," Paul said. "Should I tell them in person or by phone? What will they ask? How much do I have to tell?"

Paul decided to make it simple. He and Sofia talked first about what to say, particularly regarding his parents' relationship with Sofia and their visits with the children. He called them in the early evening, after their dinner, and told them he needed some time with them on the phone. He checked to be sure this was a good time for them to listen, and he got them both on the phone so they would hear the same thing and later be able to talk to each other about the conversation.

Paul wanted to make the following main points:

- Sofia and I have decided to get a divorce.
- I am not comfortable telling you much about our decision at this time.
- Please don't ask me any questions.
- Perhaps later I will be ready to tell you more. We are taking care of the children.
- We will make sure you get to see the children.
- I am sorry that this will be upsetting to you, but this is the best solution for me.
- I hope you will understand.
- Sofia wants to maintain a relationship with you.
- I want you to have a relationship with Sofia.
- I do not want you to denigrate her in front of the children.
- We believe we are doing what is best for us and we are working to make the decision manageable for the children.

Parents respond in many ways to the news of their children divorcing. One mother was hurt that her daughter surprised her with the news, that she did not know about the trouble from the beginning. One father became so enraged when his son quickly became involved with someone else that he disinherited his son for a time. One set of parents took their daughter-in-law's side, which was very painful for their son and he had to distance himself. Another set of parents felt shamed and kept the divorce a secret from their friends, rarely speaking of it even to each other. Feeling great pain for their children, one set of parents stayed up night after night talking long and hard about the breakup. Had they not taught their children about commitment, acceptance, and forgiveness? Should the couple have stayed together? What will happen to the grandchildren?

Parents are going to react to their child's news of divorce in all kinds of ways. That is one of the consequences of making such a large change. We cannot control what others do in response to what we do. However, we can set the stage to alleviate some of the possible negative reactions. These things can help:

- Speak calmly and politely. Ask for love and acceptance.
- Let the parents know that deciding to divorce was not an easy decision, nor is it going to change.
- Tell the parents that you have made the decision and it is the right decision.
- Ask the parents not to interfere.
- Tell the parents you would appreciate their willingness to just listen.
- Let them know some of the plans for the children, especially how you hope they, as grandparents, will be involved in the future.

Parents have an opportunity to enrich their relationship with their adult children by listening and responding as requested. If the divorcing couple does not disclose important information, then parents can voice their wishes—not to fix the relationship of the divorcing couple, but to express their feelings and to understand how they are to participate with each member of the family in the future. While I encourage parents to express their sadness, attempts to give advice or ask for decisions to be reconsidered should not be undertaken. As a parent, I am responsible only for my relationship with my children, not for any of their relationships. I want to continue talking with and loving my daughter, especially during and after a difficult divorce. If I try to intervene, I may damage my relationship with my son. I just want to be supportive.

Here are some words a parent might say:

- I am sorry you are going through this; it sounds difficult.
- This must have been a very hard decision, and brewing for years.
- I know you would not do this lightly.

- If there is anything either of us can do for you at this time, please ask.
- Know that we are interested, and when you want to talk, we will listen.
- If you have questions you want to ask us about our marriage, please do so.
- I want to see my grandchildren as much as possible. Please help make sure this is arranged.
- I love you.

Developing clear boundaries, support, and respect for the reconfigured family frees the divorcing couple from one more pressure, and the relationships that are to be ongoing have a better chance of succeeding.

Please Let Me Tell Our Friends When I Am Ready

"Please don't tell our friends that I am gay," Jake said to Margaret as they were divorcing. "Let me choose when, who, and how to tell. It is my business, after all." Jake hoped his divorce from Margaret would not set up factions among their friends. He wanted to be able to see the same friends as before, and to be with Margaret in social settings. He did not want his private issues revealed by her.

Margaret was very hurt and angry. She felt betrayed and lost. She had been planning to tell their friends about Jake's sexual preference as a way of explaining her situation. How else could she account for what was happening? She could appreciate that he might want his confidence maintained, but what was she to say? When she considered her dilemma, she tried to see Jake's point of view. What if Jake were to tell their friends about some of her private, weird habits. How would she feel? On the other hand, did she not have a right to tell the truth about the divorce? Was it not her story as well? As she pondered, she could see both sides of the issue.

Jake and Margaret talked together about the situation. Margaret said, "I need to be able to explain to people what happened. I know your homosexuality is your business, but now it is my business too. I will try to do this in a way that does not make our friends take sides." Then Margaret listened while Jake responded: "I understand your struggle. I will tell our six closest friends this week. I will let you know after I have spoken to them."

Stiff and formulaic as this resolution may have been, Jake and Margaret were able to deal with this major life shift in a way that suited them both.

Can a Divorce Be Peaceful?

Jack and Thelma had been married for ten years when they calmly separated, without acrimony. Jack was very proud they had handled the change so well. After fighting during the entire ten years, over every decision around money, sex, travel, politics, and recreational activities, Jack got an idea of how to cut though the anger. One evening he found Thelma in an odd mood, dashing around trying to do three things at once and not paying any attention to him. He waited until after dinner and then said he wanted to talk for a bit. Could they sit down together?

Jack sat near Thelma, not directly facing her but at a right angle so they could look away as needed without a clear withdrawal from contact. Jack tried to look pleasant. He felt very clear and strong. "Thelma," he asked, "where would you like to be in your life ten years from now? What would your life look like?" She appeared startled. She sat back and closed her eyes. What would she like her life to hold for her? She seldom let herself dream this way. Just getting through the week seemed an undertaking. She was already thirty-four and the years were slipping away.

Jack asked Thelma if she wanted to go first or second. Thelma wanted to go first so she would not be influenced by what Jack said. He realized that for the purest response they should write down their wishes and, after both had made a list, they could compare them. Thelma agreed. Already the air in the room was more agreeable than usual. They each got their own pen and paper and sat down to write. They gave each other thirty minutes, with the right to say when they were done. After the thirty minutes were up, they each confessed their fear of showing their list to the other. They agreed to receive these honest statements with care and respect. They decided to silently read each other's list and sit in silence for a few minutes before responding.

Thelma showed Jack her list: a home outside the city, three children, two cars, a part-time teaching job for herself, a full-time job for Jack in an organization not far from home, a savings account, a trip for two weeks each summer, food in the refrigerator, dinners at home together every night, a ping-pong table in the basement, her own washer and dryer, and part-time help for the children and the house. She felt her list was very prosaic, but given her interrupted childhood and her need for stability, the opportunity to state these wishes for her future gave Thelma a sense of relief. Although she knew Jack was not interested in any of what she had listed, she welcomed this opportunity to express her true feelings. She recognized that her dream was not bad or wrong, but was hers and did not need to be defended. This helped her to relax and feel her own clear direction for the first time in years—or perhaps ever.

Jack felt his life was about to take off in a direction that mattered more to him than he had realized. Writing was easier for him than telling his dreams to Thelma. He would have felt self-aggrandizing. Jack showed Thelma his list. He wanted first and foremost to have more time to write and to teach, not just at the nearby university but to offer his knowledge and expertise at other universities around the country. He wanted to become a leader in his field, perhaps even setting up a nonprofit institute to develop his work in theoretical physics. He did not want to be tied down by children, a need for a regular income, or a mortgage. He wanted to be able to travel, even abroad, when invited to speak. He wanted time to be alone, to be quiet and in peace, to think and allow thoughts to arise spontaneously.

"We do not belong together." Neither could remember who said the words, but what was said was all that was needed. They separated and each achieved what they had wished for that night at the end of the ten-year storm. To achieve such a peaceable divorce took honesty and respect for each other's honesty. Jack and Thelma each needed to open their heart to the other person's dreams, not to negate them as they had in the past. Their intention to behave decently with each other continued through the legal part of the divorce. They left the marriage with a full understanding that the decision had been made without rancor or shame.

How Can We Work Together to Prepare the Children for Our Divorce?

Ella had a lot of ideas about preparing her children, ages eight and ten, for her separation from Ed. She kept trying to engage him in planning what to say, but he would not participate. She knew she did not want the children to feel responsible. She wanted Ed to agree to make all visitation arrangements with her and not use the children as go-betweens. They knew friends who had done that with their children, and Ella thought it was bad for the children. She wanted to present Ed in a positive way to the children for the rest of their lives and to have Ed treat her similarly. She did not want him to move away, nor would she. But telling the children was not the only problem. She didn't know how to reach Ed so together, in a thoughtful way, they could communicate their plan to the children.

Finally, just before Ed moved out of the house, he agreed to have a conversation with the children in the way Ella had suggested. He wanted to be sure the children did not think they were unloved. He even told Ella he appreciated the thought she had given to the conversation. They told the children: "You were in no way the cause of the breakup; the problem is entirely with us. You should not be hopeful of a reconnection. We need to seek happiness away from each other. Our differences have become too hard to live with day by day. We just aren't right for each other. We are available to you at any time for questions and concerns. We want to keep your lives as steady and consistent as possible. We are here to help you through this major change." Now Ella and Ed had to make these statements become a reality for their children.

What Should We Say to the Children?

Children often don't know how to respond to their parents' divorce. Their feelings come out in odd ways. They may not want to leave the house. They may not want to go to school. They may cut themselves off from one parent. They may play parents off against each other. They may never make any reference to the divorce and the subsequent changes. To know what is going on with their children after a divorce, parents need to create openings for conversations, without pressure or insistence:

• How is this going for you?
• How is the visiting going?
• Do you want to change any of the plans?

- Do you have any questions I can answer?
- How are you finding the adjustment?

Children are often bewildered after a divorce. At first they may not respond to their parents' questions, but if the parents remain open, the children may come back later with some thoughts or questions of their own. They may never ask anything. They may wait a few days or thirty years to express their feelings about the divorce.

What Do I Tell the Children about My Love Life?

As their time of separation approached one year, Ed and Ella had another conversation about what to tell the children about their love affairs and how to introduce new people into the children's lives. "I don't want to hear about my children's sex life, nor do I want to tell them about mine," Ella told Ed. "I need to live my life without relying on my children as confidants, confessors, or peers. A child could be very confused by information about adult sexuality. I will date, and tell them I date, but I will not let anyone sleep at my apartment when the children are home until they are teenagers and I have known the man for at least a year." Ed thought these were good ideas and agreed to Ella's plan. Working this out so easily with Ed helped Ella appreciate his good side.

These kinds of conversations help each person leave with a more positive feeling for the other, which they can carry for the rest of their lives. Accepting, respectful, calm exchanges can infuse a new relationship between the divorced partners that leads to joint celebrations with the children and reasonable decision making in the future.

Will the Children Ever Talk About the Divorce with Me?

Some children never speak about or ask their parents about the divorce. Others wait for years to bring up the subject. An opening by a parent might lead to a conversation. Here are some ideas:

- I think you are old enough now to hear more of what went on with me that made me decide to end the marriage.
- Do you want to ask me anything about the divorce? I am here to answer.
- Were you left with questions about the divorce?

The child may not respond right away but these questions can keep the door open to later comments and questions. Years later children often reveal unrealistic wishes and painful memories about the divorce that surprise the parents. I have heard quotes like the following from many different people:

- I hoped at every holiday and birthday that you would get back together.
- I felt separate from my friends.
- I did not tell anyone about the divorce.
- I did not like to go to Dad's house.
- I did not like having to choose with whom to live.
- I went off with Dad when I was eight because I thought if I did not go with him, he would never get to know me. I meant to stay a year, but only at eighteen could I leave.
- I went with Mom because she promised me a horse. I am deeply embarrassed about that now.
- I wished I belonged to another family that was not broken.
- I am afraid to express my anger in a relationship.
- I felt as though I had been divorced.
- I am afraid to commit to someone else for life.

Sometimes children do not discuss their feelings about the divorce until they are older and married. As adults they may be able to put into words how they feel. If not, a parent may need to solicit feelings by asking how the children felt while the divorce was taking place.

When the child does share feelings about divorce, parents need to respond to any outpourings of feeling. They might apologize for not adequately explaining the situation and supporting the child through that difficult time. Mostly, they can listen without trying to talk away the child's feelings. Although it may be painful, parents need to accept what their children are saying and acknowledge their part in creating the situation.

When an adult child tells you how difficult the divorce was for him or her, here are some things you might say:

- I am so sorry our divorce was so hard for you.
- I wish I could have made it easy for you.
- I wish I had talked with you more.
- I was overwhelmed at the time and did not have enough compassion for you.
- I am glad we are talking about that time in our lives.
- I hope you will bring me other thoughts or feelings you have.
- I hope you will find a way to believe in the wonderful person you are and to trust yourself to fall in love and marry.
- I hope you will continue to come to me with your joy, your questions, and your difficulties.

Even Though I Am Forty, I Want to Know Why My Parents Divorced

When James was forty, his parents divorced, which catapulted him back into therapy. He knew his parents had a stormy marriage. He himself had married late, perhaps in part due to his parents' incompatibility. Since they did not stay married, how could he?

Finally, James got up his courage and called his parents, Tony and Rosalie. He told them that for his own peace of mind he needed more understanding of what went wrong in their marriage. He promised them their conversation would remain confidential. His parents had been rather quiet about their divorce, hoping no one would ask much. They felt a great deal of shame over marrying, having children, and then waiting so long to separate. They told James they had married when they were young so Tony could become a U.S. citizen. Rosalie soon found herself pregnant, despite their plans to separate early. They stayed together for the sake of the children. Tony worked long hours because he had nothing to look forward to at home with Rosalie. They did not fight, and they did not talk. They had no interests in common, and they each felt the other had stolen their life. After the children left home, Tony and Rosalie tried to find things to do together, but more and more, they spent time apart. Tony wanted to retire and move to Florida, but Rosalie did not want to leave her close friends in Rochester. They decided to separate.

Tony and Rosalie were relieved to tell James the truth. James now understood better his own struggles with intimacy, and he was relieved that the dissolution was in no way his fault, nor had he missed big signs of dissension in his household. Airing the truth helped everyone.

Not all separations are as rational as Tony and Rosalie's. The divorce of Melody's parents led to a considerable amount of pain. Her parents were very distant from each other for years. Her father was the heart of the family. After all the children left home, he moved out, too, to marry another woman who had been in his life for a long time. The added pain in this divorce was that Hilda, the new wife, did not want Melody's father to stay involved with his first family, and he obeyed her wishes. He disappeared into another life. He lived for only nine years after the divorce, and Melody saw him just a few times during those years, always at her initiative. When they did meet, they needed to choose a location away from his house.

Melody wished her father had made her more of a priority. Why did he not stand up to his new wife? Why was Hilda's anxiety more important to him than the feelings of his daughter? During one of their infrequent meetings, she finally asked him what had allowed this to happen. "I am hurt that you have allowed Hilda to keep us apart all these years," she said. "What has the separation from me been like for you?"

And then she listened. Her father apologized to her and begged her forgiveness. All he had to say was, "I wish I had not done that to you. I don't know what I was so afraid of." Melody's father's response did not make up for all the lost years of being without her father, but it helped.

The adult children in both these examples requested more information, and their need to know prompted the parents to answer. The initiation of the conversation could have come from either the parents or the adult children.

How Can I Reach Out to My Children Years after My Divorce?

After Jerry and Lena split up, Jerry was overwhelmed by the changes in his life and took his questions to a therapist. He felt himself spiraling downward with the unanswerable question, "Who am I now?" To clear up the muddle in his mind, he needed someone to listen while he reflected back over the years of his marriage. The therapist was supportive, not judgmental, and he allowed Jerry to come to conclusions rather than giving advice. He listened as no one ever had before. The therapist used his own life's hard times to find ways to respond to Jerry. He helped Jerry understand how some of the things Jerry told himself about being unlovable were not based in fact. Jerry began to feel less alone and more interested in his future. He began to see his part in the breakup—and Lena's part as well.

Jerry realized, from talking with the therapist, that if he wanted his grown children in his life, he would have to reach out to them. First, he needed to say three simple but hard-to-say words: "I am sorry." To each one, he said he was sorry he had left them when he left their mother. He let them know that he was sorry he had not spent much time with them as children. He told them of his intention to find ways to be with them. He began calling them each week and asking about their life and their work. He listened to their answers. He talked about himself, his joys and sorrows.

This was new for Jerry. He made plans to take time off work to travel and meet with each of his children. He found he liked them. They had interesting conversations. They were at similar points in their lives in some respects. Jerry met his children's friends. He was taken into their lives in ways he never expected. His children seemed to accept and appreciate him as he was. They shared some funny memories of childhood. He began to feel alive. His children needed him in some way. Tomorrow was less threatening to him now, with his children in his life.

Conclusion

With conscious effort, thoughtfulness, and a respect for the long-term consequences, couples can divorce without damaging each other. If two people share a belief that behaving decently is better in the long run for themselves and their family, they will find a way to amicably dissolve their partnership. In turn this will allow them and their children to go on and enter into other loving relation-ships. With time many former couples are able to feel comfortable with each other in the same room. This means they are able to cel-ebrate holidays, birthdays, and their children's milestones together. Achieving this degree of civility takes effort, thoughtfulness, and the motivation of doing it for the children.

CHAPTER 7

Learning to Be Adults with Each Other— Parents and Adult Children

Many books have been written for parents about how to talk to small children and adolescents. Rarely is attention directed to the difficulties that arise between adult children and their parents. Some parents treat their adult children as if they still require rearing and protection. Some adult children continue to see their parents as larger than life, while others may see their parents as irrelevant. Spending some time balancing these perceptions can lead to a fulfilling, open relationship that is nourishing and growth inducing for all those involved. As children grow into adults who are faced with the responsibilities of professional life, home life, and child rearing, they begin to see their parents as people who dealt with similar issues, from whom they can learn. Many realize their parents may need support but they can also give support. And parents of adult children have a great opportunity to watch, support, enjoy, and delight in the talents and strengths that are appearing in their adult children. The best outcome is when both generations enjoy spending time together.

During the transition a child makes from home into the world, new areas can be discussed to enhance the connection between the generations. Here are some suggested topics:

- Leaving home gracefully.
- Expressing needs without becoming heated and divisive.
- Respecting privacy.
- Being supportive and at the same time being able to back off.
- Accepting the different values and perspectives of each generation.
- Caring for but not being caught up with each other to the point of discomfort.
- Determining the amount and duration of financial assistance.
- Sharing costs on family vacations.

By exploring the efforts of others as they found their way through the thicket of potential controversies, a multi-generational family can learn different ways to interact gently with each other.

How Can I Get My Son to Talk to Me?

"I have one child who does not tell me what I want to know. I need to know about his health, but he keeps me in the dark." My friend Larry told me about this situation as we walked down Broadway toward the New York City theater district. We were going to a play about a family, which brought up the same issues he was dealing with in his own life. Larry did not want to lose contact with his son, Barnaby, who was living in Portugal. Barnaby has asthma, which is not always effectively controlled by medication. From New York, Larry had no way of knowing how his son was or whether he was doing all he could to stay well. Larry knew he couldn't protect his son from this ailment, and was alternating between quiet acceptance and the desire to help in some way. Larry told me that he did not like waking up at night worrying. While knowing that worrying does no good, he would still wake up worrying. "What if Barnaby, who lives alone, has breathing trouble? What if he gets to the hospital and can't be understood? What if, what if? Toss and turn. What did I do that he moved so far away? What if he stays in Portugal forever?"

As we walked, I thought about what my friend was telling me. I learned that Barnaby tells his father about his new research project, his new girlfriend's family, his daily life, even about the food he eats. But he never mentions his health, the one thing Larry wants most to know about. Then I thought about my relationship with my parents—what I did and did not tell them and how often I postponed telling them the things of importance that they really wanted to know about. I did not disclose to my parents even half as much as Barnaby was telling Larry. I was trying to be independent and self-sufficient. I did not want to need parents. I was a grown-up. Was Barnaby likewise struggling for his adulthood?

I asked Larry what he had told his parents when he was in his twenties and thirties. He replied, "Nothing," and laughed.

Several months later, Larry told me that he was trying to be less hooked into health reports from Barnaby. He was now trusting that if he needed to know something, his son would tell him. He felt at first as though he were a less-than-good father because he did not worry as much, but after a time he let go of that too. When Larry felt looser about Barnaby's asthma, he said to his son: "I trust that you will let me know if you have trouble with your asthma. I know you know how to take care of yourself. I love you. That is why I want to know how you are." Larry pointed out that he had not asked about Barnaby's health in months and that he wanted credit for that. He told Barnaby that he could understand not wanting to be quizzed about his asthma on every call, but that as his father he would like to know the ups and downs of Barnaby's health. He knew he could do nothing from New York, but as his father, he would just feel more at ease if he knew what was really happening. Larry also promised that he would try not to ask too often and that he hoped Barnaby would keep him informed.

Larry was reassured when Barnaby said he had minimal difficulty during all his time in Portugal, that he felt good about how he had handled the difficult moments, and that he had not meant to keep anything from his father. Barnaby's response made Larry realize that he was a worrier. He felt better after talking to Barnaby about his feelings, relieved that Barnaby did not react by cutting him off. Most of all, he was relieved that Barnaby was caring for himself so well.

Why Do They Tell Me These Things?

Some adult children are very private in conversation with their parents, telling only the minimum about their life and not seeming to welcome questions. On the other hand, I have talked with several parents lately who wish their adult children would stop telling them about misbehavior in the distant past or business problems in the present. One son told his parents about his drug use in high school. A daughter told her mother about her dating style in college, confessing that she would often go out with more than one boy in one night, which was not consistent with the mother's values or with what the mother thought she knew about her daughter. Another son talked about frequently skipping classes. Learning about the ups and downs of a child's fledgling business keeps one parent up at night, when worrying will not make a difference. These tales of past exploits and current problems can leave parents feeling guilty about their parenting, ashamed of what their child did, and wishing they did not have to know at this point.

In each case, the parent was perplexed about just how to respond. They did not want to shut down the intimate, trusting connection that seemed to be blooming. Several of the parents wanted to say, "I don't need to hear about what happened long ago. I feel upset by this information." But they continued to listen, despite their discomfort, afraid they might otherwise seem to be condoning dishonesty.

What else might a parent say in this kind of situation?

- I am glad you are so open with me at this point in your life, but sometimes I end up feeling quite uncomfortable after these disclosures.
- What is it you are hoping to hear from me? A solution, absolution, or just that I listen?
- What brings this up now?
- Did I respond to you the way you would have liked me to respond?

One man told his daughter that he disapproved of her past behavior. He said she had used very poor judgment in eleventh grade when she had smoked marijuana during school hours. Later he realized his censure was a little late, and he apologized. One woman, after hearing about her son's business problems in response to "How are you?" became so concerned that she told him to let her know when the problem had been resolved. "I'm a worrier. You have told me about your trouble at work, so please tell me when the problem has been solved. Otherwise, I will keep worrying."

One son wanted to talk about his business problems with his parents but needed to feel he had the ability to resolve them in his own way, without his parents' advice, and not necessarily using the method or time frame that would suit them. The parents learned to listen and, when the issue was resolved, to tell their son:

- I hope this is what you wanted.
- I am glad you came to a decision.
- I am very pleased you got what you wanted.

- I trust you are happy.
- I am excited; I hope you are.

Why Does My Daughter Talk More to Her Aunt Than to Me?

Kara does not tell her mother anything. She talks to her aunt. She even stays at her aunt's house when she goes to Atlanta. Kara is now living in New York, and her mother, Alice, longs to know about her life, especially about who she is dating. But Kara feels invaded by her mother's questions and so she dodges them. She can talk and talk and talk with Aunt Sally, who does not respond with questions or judgments. Support and pleasure are what she gets from Sally. In fact, she can't wait to go to Sally's and sit down with a pot of tea for one of their long talks.

What prevents Kara from teaching her mother to listen to her the way she wants to be listened to? What prevents Alice from asking her sister, Sally, or even Kara, what she might do to be taken into Kara's confidence? To open the door to conversation Alice could ask Kara some questions:

- I am interested in knowing how you are doing,
- I am interested in hearing anything you would like to tell me.
- I would like to listen and respond in a way that works for both of us.
- What do I do that bothers you?
- I need your help.

Or Kara could say to her mother:

- I just want you to listen to me.
- I don't want advice or even questions.
- I want to end our conversation feeling that what I have told you is confidential, that what I say is just between us.

* I want your support or your neutrality.
* I don't want to feel judged by you.
* I want to be able to be open with you, but sometimes I feel that what I say may be used against me later. I don't feel safe.
* I would like to listen to you talk about your day and your ups and downs so we are more like two friends talking to each other.

Alice and Kara were able to talk about their estrangement, but after Kara revealed her true feelings, Alice felt very contrite and was cautious for a while in conversations with Kara. She had not wanted to be the kind of mother who judges and picks on her daughter. Seeing herself that way was painful. She decided to let Kara take the lead in conversations, and from time to time, she asked for feedback on how she was doing. This was startling to Kara, but she appreciated it. Sometimes before asking her nosier questions, Alice would say, "I am going ask you about something that is none of my business, so please tell me to stop when you need to."

What Can I Say When My Adult Child Is Angry with Me?

Dorothy moved to Rome after college, leaving her mother, who had been a single parent, in Maine. A few months after arriving in Rome, Dorothy went into therapy for the first time and began examining who she was and what was holding her back from becoming her fullest self. In the therapy sessions, she allowed herself to express anger at her mother for the first time. She had always been afraid of this emotion because her mother was all she had.

During their next phone conversation, Dorothy very politely began telling her mother she was angry that her mother had kept her young for so long. She had not been allowed to go to pajama parties or to date when her friends were dating. She was angry she had to be home at 10 p.m. on weekends.

"It's okay for you to be angry," her mother told Dorothy. "You don't need to protect me." She told her daughter that she knew they loved each other and that mothers were often hard for daughters to accept and enjoy. She wanted Dorothy to be open with her.

Dorothy was relieved by this statement and learned to express her anger about past incidents in therapy and to address her mother with current issues only as they arose. When Dorothy came home for the first visit, she was annoyed that her mother seemed to think she was home to stay. Her mother made several comments suggesting that enough was enough; the time had come to end the European exploration. Finally, with her newfound courage, Dorothy said, "Mother, I hear that you wish I was living near you and that you are happy I am home now, but I am going back to Rome. I love you and I miss you, and I want to continue talking with you on the phone each week. Living and studying in Rome is very good for me."

Her mother listened carefully to what Dorothy was telling her. She could hear her own words through her daughter's ears. Then she apologized, recognizing that she was, indeed, trying to impose her own agenda. After that conversation, Dorothy felt relaxed when she called home, and she looked forward to future visits with more pleasure.

How Can I Get My Parents to Listen to How I Am Feeling?

"When my brother was abusing alcohol and stealing from my parents," June told me, "they listened to me and cared about me. But now that Roger is living a productive life, he seems to be getting all the attention and money. They have even changed their will to favor him." June was hurt and angry. She had taken a lot of verbal abuse from her parents when she was young. She did not want to confront them and stir up their old behavior. However, she needed to speak up. She said, speaking from the hurt not the anger, "I am feeling poorly treated by you lately. I am hurt that you have given Roger so much money and changed your will to support him more than me. I thought you said you would give more to me in your will because you have given so much to him in the past."

They were angry with June for being a greedy, self-seeking girl who did not sympathize with Roger, considering all he had been through. As an adult, June was able to tell her parents that she did not see herself this way, and she was sorry they did. June felt she had made no difference in the way her parents were going to treat her, but she did stop burning inside. Having taken an active step on her own behalf, she had a sense of release from no longer having to silently carry this grievance inside of her.

How Does a Mother Ask for What She Wants?

After several months of treatment, at age eighty-five Maria chose to discontinue the medical fight against her ovarian cancer. At that point Alba, Maria's out-of-town daughter, decided to visit for a month. Alba did not ask her mother whether she wanted her to come or not. Maria liked her privacy and she was accustomed to caring for herself. She was embarrassed at not wanting her daughter to stay with her for so long a time. Maria had many friends who would be helping her. She had arranged for hospice care at her doctor's suggestion, and she wanted some quiet time to reflect. She did not know how to tell her daughter she wanted her there at the end of her life, not right now, so she decided to endure the visit.

Four days into her daughter's visit, Maria decided she had to talk with Alba before she became any weaker. She told Alba how pleased she was about the visit and that Alba would be a big help. Maria told her she was still feeling well enough to do some things for herself. "It is important for me to remain independent as long as possible," she said, "and to have time to think back on my life." Maria had a schedule set up of who was coming to visit when, and while Alba was welcome to join them, she encouraged Alba to make arrangements to go out with some of her childhood friends, at least while Maria was still up and about.

After a few days Alba and Maria fell into a comfortable rhythm with each other. Maria even felt she could say to Alba, "I am going to my room now to think and read. I will see you at dinnertime." Alba read, visited with friends, and helped with meals. The women found a very companionable place to be together. Maria let go of her fear that she was not going to have any time alone before she died, and she was able to appreciate deeply her daughter's presence when they were together. As for Alba, she found that her mother, at this time in her life, was no longer critical or demanding, as she'd been in the past. The two women enjoyed their month together, even driving out to the beach a few times to sit in the car with the wind blowing and the birds calling. Alba was able to thank Maria for giving her the eyes and ears with which to see, hear, and enjoy the birds wherever she went.

In this case, if Maria had told her daughter not to come, or to come for only a week, the unfolding of their renewed relationship would never have taken place. Making sure they had time apart as well as time together allowed them to enjoy each other with ease.

When Do Daughters Get to Express Their Needs?

Carolyn told me that she and her daughter Roxie have a wonderful telephone relationship. They speak to each other a few times a week and get along famously. But when her daughter visits, Carolyn feels that she gets on her daughter's nerves, and Roxie is short with her, often saying: "'I know that already, Mother. You don't have to tell me." "Roxie criticizes me," Carolyn said. "'Your shoes are shabby.

Your blouse has spots. I think you aren't taking care of yourself as you should.' What business is it of hers? She has a life. I don't go to her house and tell her how to clean or where to put things. I must be doing something wrong that she is so short with me, but I don't know what. I love her very much and I would like to have her visit more often, but once she gets here, I feel her pulling away from me. I think I need to talk to her."

In a support-group setting, we discussed what Carolyn might say to open a conversation with Roxie:

- You sound angry with me.
- Have I offended you?
- What do you need from me at this point in your life?
- I love having you here, but I get the feeling you are uncomfortable about something.
- Learning to be two women together is difficult, especially because we are mother and daughter.
- What can I do to make our visits easier?

When Roxie visited next, Carolyn asked her daughter some of these questions. Roxie listened and then told her mother she appreciated the opening her mother had given her. She said she did not want to sound critical, but some things Carolyn did bothered her and maybe if they talked about these things, they would get along better. Roxie felt that her mother's complaints about her aging, her health, and the decisions she had to make were meant to suggest that Roxie could make everything all right for her. Roxie felt her mother's dependence on her like a heavy weight, which made her feel angry and helpless.

Carolyn acknowledged that perhaps she did want Roxie to fix things for her. She was not simply airing her concerns. At the same time, Carolyn admitted that she could not expect her daughter to be responsible for her life.

Roxie was greatly relieved to hear this from Carolyn, but she still had to try to get out of this reactive cycle. Roxie decided that whenever she felt guilty about something her mother said, she was going to say, "Life is so hard." She would tell her mother that she heard her discomfort and, at the same time, she was not there to fix it. Roxie also learned to say: "I can't do this for you, Mom. I would like to help more but I am busy with my own life now. I don't like feeling guilty about your situation."

Carolyn was able to accept this, since she felt heard. Roxie maintained her freedom. And each of them, mother and daughter, felt better than they had in a long time.

How Can I Get More from My Father?

My friend Annabelle, who is in her forties, confessed to me that she finds her father's visits and phone calls boring. He never says anything about himself. He asks her only the most perfunctory questions, such as "How are you doing?" but he does not seem to want much of an answer. She feels cut off before she begins and can't think of anything to talk to her father about. "My father does not know how to relate," she says. "He has always been hard to reach."

Roger, Annabelle's father, was widowed as a young man and left with four children. He was stricken by his wife's death but worked hard to provide for his family. A number of relatives helped him raise the children. Now in the last phase of his life, he seems to be reaching out to Annabelle, but does not know how to connect with her. Heartfelt conversation was not part of his growing up, and he did not have enough time with his wife to learn how to share his feelings. Now he wants a relationship with Annabelle, but he does not know what to say.

I suggested to Annabelle that she teach her father the language of intimacy. She could begin cautiously, talking with him about her own bad days and good days, events that make her feel less than good, times when she is upset by criticism, times when she wishes she had acted differently. She might tell him about events in her life that give her pleasure. From these conversations Roger might learn what to ask her and what to tell her about himself.

Annabelle might say:

- I hate to complain but someone at work ...
- This job is a very good situation for me, and here is why.
- I feel sort of down today. You don't need to fix it. I just want to say how I feel out loud.
- I am very happy about how things are going with Luke, my new boyfriend.
- Last weekend Luke and I went skiing.

Or she might ask her father questions and make some comments:

- How are you doing today? (This is a small, active question that is not asking for emotions.)
- Do you still like to fish, golf, read, walk [whatever was his pleasure]?
- I remember the time we went to the boat show together.
- Tell me about your parents [brothers, cousins].
- What are you proud of in your life? Recently?

These prompts could help Annabelle through several phone calls. One question can stir up another. People usually have childhood stories they want to tell.

- What did you do as a kid?
- What did you get in trouble for when you were young?
- When did you leave home?
- What was your first job?

- How did you decide to work at ... ?
- How did you decide to live in ... ?

As they begin to share more of their lives, Annabelle might want to broach more intimate subjects. She could talk about her memories of her mother, and then ask her father:

- What was Mother like when you met her?
- How did you meet her?
- What did she like to do?
- What made you love her?
- How did you feel when she was sick?
- How did you feel when she died?

Annabelle knows how to open up and express herself with her friends. She could model that behavior for her father. She would enjoy the conversations with her father more if she were saying more, and then maybe someday she would hear more from him. Perhaps he will find the words to share his life with her. Then the two might have a meaningful relationship in which love and wisdom are exchanged, and Annabelle might have one true parent instead of none.

How Do I Handle My Disapproval of My Daughter?

When my friend Andrea was visiting, I asked about her daughter. "Rhonda has finally moved out," Andrea told me. "Two grown women sharing my house was not working. Rhonda has a job. She has moved with a few other people outside of town, where they are fixing up an old farmhouse."

I remembered Rhonda as a rebellious teenager, and I was surprised that after college she returned to Oakland, got a job, and lived with her mother. The three years since graduation had not been easy. The two women hardly talked, and when they did they were barely civil. Andrea reported that Rhonda was dating a man who was unemployed, and he was moving to the farm as well. Although Rhonda's new boyfriend was not someone Andrea would have chosen for her daughter, she told me she was not expressing her displeasure. I told Andrea I thought she was very wise and asked her how she knew to be quiet in this situation. Andrea said that when she was young, she had brought home unusual and unseemly young men just to bug her parents, and she assumed Rhonda was doing that now. If she were to express her true feelings, she would further alienate Rhonda, possibly pushing her into the arms of the young man and injuring her precarious relationship with her daughter. Andrea hoped that if she stayed out of the picture, Rhonda would figure out for herself that she could find a more suitable boyfriend.

Andrea wished she could direct her daughter's life, but she knew from her own experience the value of making mistakes and finding one's own way. She wanted to give Rhonda the chance to do that. Andrea hoped she would watch her daughter grow more mature, but Andrea was also afraid that after Rhonda moved to the farm, she might not stay in touch with her mother. Because the last three years had been so acrimonious, now that they were living apart Andrea wanted to talk with Rhonda about their relationship. She thought about saying:

- Over the last few years there has been a lot of anger between us, but I want you to know I love you and always will.
- I hope we will stay in touch. Please give me your phone number and let's talk about how often we might talk to each other.
- Do you want me to call you? Or do you want to call me?
- Would you rather e-mail?
- Do you want to come home sometimes?
- Do you want to wait for an invitation?

* If you want to visit, I will be thrilled. Just let me know ahead of time so I can be with you when you are here.
* I will miss you. I hope we can be together again with ease after we live apart.
* Would you like me to visit you at the farm when you are set up?
* I think this is a great move for you.
* In a few weeks let's make a date to go shopping for stuff for your new place.
* I will miss you, and I will be fine here without you.
* I know these past few years have not been easy.

Andrea wanted to avoid a complete rupture with her daughter. She rehearsed with me to prepare for a successful conversation with Rhonda. When she spoke to Rhonda, Andrea was surprised that Rhonda became teary and thanked her mother for caring so much. Rhonda said she would stay in touch. She called home weekly and let her mother know how she was doing. She seldom asked for advice; mostly she recounted the events of her week. From time to time the two women went shopping and to the movies, and Rhonda learned that her mother did not voice opinions about her life. Rhonda grew more comfortable in her presence and with time realized that Andrea was one of the easiest people in her life to talk with. Andrea had learned to listen and not to advise unless asked directly. Rhonda now shared with her mother her disappointments, her successes, her hopes, and her plans to achieve them.

How Can I Help My Adult Children Talk to Each Other?

Although they are siblings, Chloe and Ruford are very different. Born eight years apart, they seemed to have grown up in different families. Their mother, Sandy, went back to work full time when

Ruford was three months old, whereas she had stayed home with Chloe. Gil, their father, tried to fill in for Sandy by driving some carpools, buying party gifts, and organizing sitters, but Ruford had much less parental time than Chloe. When Ruford was born, Chloe was already in school; by seventeen she had left home. When the children were in their twenties, Sandy and Gil found getting them to come home for Thanksgiving and other holidays was difficult. Friends suggested they plan a vacation that neither child could resist and see what might happen. Gil and Sandy liked this idea. They looked for a place where each of them had some independence, where all meals did not need to be eaten communally, and where there would be an opportunity for family time. Renting a house on the west coast of Costa Rica was within their means, and offered water sports and inland sightseeing, which Chloe and Ruford both enjoyed. A little nightlife was available at two restaurants. Some family members could eat in town or they could all have a meal together in one location or another.

Not wanting to have a hidden agenda with their children, after Ruford and Chloe agreed to go to Costa Rica Gil and Sandy said to them:

- I am aware that you have not spent time with Ruford [Chloe] in a long time.
- I am hoping you will get to know him [her] during this week together.
- We care about both of you and think you would like each other.
- I am glad we are taking this time to be together.
- I hope when you need a break from family time you will find a way to go somewhere for a few hours and rejoin us refreshed.
- I want you to be aware of some of what instigated this trip.
- If there are unspoken difficulties between you, I hope you will raise these with Chloe [Ruford].

• If you want to go off together in the evenings, that is fine.
• We don't have to be together all the time.

Gil and Sandy talked to each other about their expectations. They realized that while they could set the stage for a rapprochement between their children, they could not make anything happen. They acknowledged the risk of a blow up and they talked about the value of accepting whatever may come. "The children are now adults, and they can make of their time what they will," Sandy said to Gil. Keeping a positive attitude toward their time together with no attachment to the results was how they could best set the stage for a pleasant family reunion.

Conclusion

As children grow up, move out, and find their way in the world, they also find their voices. As children move on, parents need to speak to their offspring with a respect that recognizes their growing autonomy. New issues arise when children leave home and even when they return home for extended periods of time. Taking time to talk, without running away from the charged issues, moves the growth process along. The development of the adult child needs to be taken into consideration, as well as the establishment of a new kind of relationship between adults of more than one generation. For parents one of the satisfactions of middle age is the joy of finding out who their adult children have become. In return, adult children have an opportunity to see their parents without the larger-than-life childhood image. To move toward a place of trust, respect, acceptance, and pleasure is part of the unfolding of this stage of family life.

CHAPTER 8

Watching Married Adult Children
Find Their Own Way

Another phase in the ever-evolving relationship between the generations comes when adult children marry and in-laws enter the picture. At this time the nuclear family expands; the wives of sons and the husbands of daughters arrive, bringing parents the opportunity to know and love more people. Getting to know a new family member while respecting the relationship of the newlyweds and the relationship between the generations takes consciousness and care, just as the other relationships described in this book. And along with the pleasure of a growing family, new issues tend to arise as adult children begin to define their lifestyle. They are melding their values and practices with another person. Sometimes adult children are outspoken in defense of their way; sometimes parents expect their way to rule even in the new household. Often not enough is said and negative feelings fester. Respect again plays a part in keeping these relationships on an even keel.

How Can I Ask My Mother for Help?

When Rob and Aden were in their twenties, with two small babies at home, Aden died suddenly of an aneurysm. Rob's mother came to help as soon as she heard the news. Three days after the funeral, she said, "I am going home now; I don't want you to become dependent on me." Rob collapsed internally at the news. At that time he was not able to say, "Stay. I need you. Badly." He too was distressed by his dependence on his mother. Rob was frightened, lonely, and tired, so he let his mother leave.

Rob's mother was feeling overwhelmed by the tragic situation. She had raised four children, but now, after ten years without children at home, she had her days to herself to garden and visit friends. She was afraid of losing herself in the domestic turmoil of Rob's household and worried that she would never be able to leave if she did not pull away now. She knew that Rob would become more capable as the days went by. She could not really face thinking about Rob's needs, so great was her need to return to her quiet life.

Now, thirty years later, Rob is still amazed that his mother left him when he obviously needed her. If Rob had been stronger, he told me, he would have asked his mother to stay. He regrets accepting his mother's decision to leave without expressing his own needs, but expressing his needs was difficult for him at that point in his life. If only someone had told him that having needs is okay. If he had been able to talk to his mother, she might have changed her mind and responded to his need or she might have left anyway. Either way at least Rob would have known that he had asked for the help he obviously needed.

What might Rob have said to his mother when she announced she was leaving?

- Mother, can we talk about your decision?
- I am dependent right now, but I will learn to run this household with your help.
- Mother, I need you.
- This is hard for me to say, but please stay for a few weeks.
- I appreciate so much what you have done for me, and I don't think I can do this without you. Please stay.

- I know you are feeling overwhelmed by my household, and I will help you all I can, but I need you to stay.

Rob told me that because of what happened with his mother so long ago, he always asks his adult children if they need help when babies arrive, when they move, and when someone is sick:

- Do you want me to come and help? I would like to do that.
- How long would you like me to stay?
- Will you please tell me to leave when you are ready to be on your own?
- Will you please ask me to stay when you think I am leaving too early?

Telling others that we need them is often difficult. We feel weak and vulnerable, which is uncomfortable. But in some situations, like Rob's, we truly are overwhelmed and must ask for help. Although Rob was not able to talk with his mother years ago, he eventually learned to ask for help with his four children, and he learned how to offer himself to his children and their families.

What Can I Say to My Father about His Broken Promises?

William does not know what to do about his father. His father calls to say he is coming to visit and William clears the weekend. Daisy, age three, gets excited about seeing her grandpa, but then he cancels, or he comes but leaves earlier than promised. One time when William's father called to say he was sending Daisy a birthday gift, William burst out, "I will tell her when I see the gift and not before. I don't want her to suffer over your broken promises." William felt ashamed the moment these words left his lips, but he was determined to protect his daughter, even if he did not protect himself.

His father was crushed. He loved William, and their relationship was one of the few good things remaining in his life. Daisy gave him great pleasure. He wanted to visit his son and granddaughter, but he did not want to be a nuisance. He dreaded sitting around with this smart, successful, productive family, trying to think of things to say and feeling inadequate. They lived a life he knew nothing about. He had grown up in a household where Thanksgiving had been silent and Christmas had been acrimonious. How could he know what to say? How could he ask intelligent questions about their lives and their work? It was easier to cancel. William would be relieved, he told himself.

William considered talking to his father but decided against it. While thinking about the situation, William realized that, given who his dad was, he had to let go of his expectations of him. That his father wanted to come and see him would have to be enough. Any change had to be in himself, in his expectations of his father. William toned down his desire to have his father appear when he said he would, but he didn't stop inviting him to visit. He invited him and then let go. William felt much better after he was able to do this a few times.

Five years later, the situation continued. His father's behavior—changing plans, not doing what he said he would do—was again upsetting William. This time William told his father about his hurt—not his anger. He did not ask *why* questions, knowing that *why* implies the other person is wrong and tends to induce guilt and carry blame. Instead, William spoke about his own internal reaction to his father's unpredictable behavior. William had thought about the conversation beforehand and realized that his father would get defensive if William acted angrily. He wanted to be able to talk about keeping one's word without either of them saying harsh words. He realized ahead of time that if he avoided the word *anger* and instead expressed his feelings of hurt, he had a better chance of getting a thoughtful response from his father. Although he did not need a response, a response would be nice. What he really needed was to share his feelings.

The next time William's father called, William said, "Dad, I don't want to make a big thing of this, but I want you to know that I've feel let down when you say you're coming to visit and then you don't. I'm really feeling disappointed and hurt." William did not talk long. He quietly and briefly stated his problem.

His father was dumbfounded. He had not realized he was causing pain. He thought everyone was relieved when he did not come to visit. After this conversation, William's father improved a little in following through on his word, but even more important, William felt he handled the situation well. He had spoken honestly and directly to his father, communicating his own feelings about the situation without saying anything unkind.

What Is a Mother-in-Law's Business?

As a psychotherapist I met with Laura after she had several miscarriages. Laura told Rochelle, her mother-in-law, that she was starting to take hormones to try to maintain a pregnancy. Laura also told Rochelle that in the future she might consider additional medical interventions. Rochelle received the news and waited to hear more. For a year she asked nothing, although she found this to be difficult. She did not know if her son and daughter-in-law had given up on trying to have a child of their own or how they were feeling about the situation. She also knew this was not quite her business, but knowing nothing for so long, she worried.

Rochelle talked with a friend about the situation, explaining that because she'd had no news for a year, the issue had grown huge for her. Her friend suggested that since Laura had already mentioned the hormone treatment, they might have a conversation in which Rochelle opened by saying:

- I think about your desire for a baby from time to time. When you have news about a baby, I trust you will tell me. I am open to hearing the good and the bad news.
- I have not heard anything for a year. I just want to know a little of what is happening now.
- I know your struggle with pregnancy is not my business, but I hope you will share your baby news with me, as you did in the past.

Laura replied that she had no news but she hoped soon to have something to report—and Rochelle would be one of the first to hear.

What Can I Say When My Parents Tell Me How to Raise My Children?

Teresa and Ernst, who did not want to raise their children the way they had been raised, were politically more radical than their parents, and were also open to nontraditional forms of activity and association. They allowed their children more latitude in choosing friends and after-school programs. At the same time Teresa and Ernst did not want their parents to feel their values were being dismissed. But a collision of values did occur.

Although Teresa and Ernst lived a thousand miles away from their original homes, their parents called and visited often. The older generation wanted to maintain an active relationship with their grandchildren, but they openly commented on the state of the household, offered opinions on everything, and often indicated displeasure. Why do our grandchildren play soccer rather than tennis, attend public instead of private schools, have no religious affiliation, take drama and art classes instead of piano and dance? Surprisingly, all four grandparents shared the same opinions and were equally willing to express them.

What might Teresa and Ernst say to their parents to show their respect while not giving up their personal preferences for their children? They might say:

- We respect the methods you used to raise us and would like you to give us the opportunity to raise our children our way.

- What you did for us was fine, but Teresa and I are different people and can't follow completely in your footsteps.

- None of us makes perfect decisions for our children. We need to follow our way and learn from our own mistakes.

- You have given us so much: the freedom to think, an awareness of the need to be conscious and careful in making decisions about our children, the ability to love our children and be delighted with each child's particular passion. We would not have any of this without you.

- We would not be the successful people we are today without you.

- We are using a great deal of what we learned from you in raising our children.

- Let us look at the similarities instead of the differences.

- We all treat children with respect.

- We all teach them to interact with adults.

- We all care about education.

- We all want them to be fed and housed and have some routine.

- We all care about good food and pleasant surroundings.

- We all put the health and development of our children above all other considerations.

- We care about healthy minds, bodies, and spirits, even though we do this in different ways.

- Let us rejoice together in the wonder of these children.

First, Teresa spoke with her parents. They surprised her by agreeing completely that she was the one to decide about her children's development. After their conversation, Teresa realized that her parents were indeed supportive of her and wanted her to live her life her way. She had made assumptions about them that were wrong. Her parents stopped pushing their opinions and ideas.

Ernst's parents, on the other hand, said, "Yes, yes, yes," and then continued with the same comments: "Don't you think the children should ... ?" "I think it would be a good idea if ... and I will pay." "I think you are making a big mistake by ..." Ernst was frustrated. He decided each time they offered advice, he would remind them that he was the parent—that they had had their turn. He also considered saying they had done a great job and he wanted to do a great—but slightly different—job. Ernst's work with his parents was going to continue. He would have to have the same conversation with them again—and perhaps many times after that. And he knew he was having the conversation with his parents he needed to have.

How Do I Learn to Be a Good In-Law?

The wedding of Gerald and Nina was an evening of joy, dancing, and glowing love. Pauline, Gerald's mother, arrived at the going-away brunch the next morning and realized she was now a mother-in-law. Pauline thought about her neighbor Helen, who had a mother-in-law with too many ideas about how Helen should care for her children. Helen resented her mother-in-law's suggestions. She talked to Pauline about how reduced, wronged, and judged she felt. The advice usually made Helen want to do the opposite of what was recommended. After many years of suffering her mother-in-law's intrusion, Helen had felt compelled to say to her, "This time I need you to let me rearrange our living room my way. This change is very important to me." Surprisingly, her mother-in-law realized Helen had her own way of caring for the house and apologized. After years of protecting the older woman from Helen's true feelings, Helen became a person with her own views in her mother-in-law's eyes. And after hearing about Helen's in-law problems, Pauline often called and asked Helen's advice about decisions in her own life.

With every wedding, family members take on new roles—bride, groom, mother-in-law, father-in-law—representing changes in relationships that need attention. Sometimes everyone celebrates the marriage, a new family member is accepted, and the family harmoniously grows. But too often toes are crushed feelings are hurt, and regrets arise about things said or unsaid. In too many families resentment begins to grow and, if unattended, may continue throughout life.

Pauline did not know in the first months of being a mother-in-law how useful spending time with Nina, her new daughter-in-law, might have been. She later wished she had told Nina to let her know when she stepped on her toes and when she voiced opinions that were not her business. Sometimes when Pauline visited she was too helpful. She bustled around, cleaning the sink, folding laundry, and fixing the beds. She forgot her own experiences as a young bride when she had felt quite burdened by her parents' visits. With her constant "helping," Pauline's mother had made her feel that she was not competent. As a result, Pauline had promised herself that she would not clean around anyone else's stove with a toothbrush, but she found herself constantly jumping up off the couch to try to relieve Nina of some of the repetitious domestic jobs.

Finally, Gerald and Nina had to intervene. They told Pauline that while they appreciated her help, she was doing too much.

If Pauline had asked some questions in the beginning, she would not have been brought to a polite halt by her children. She might have said:

- When either of us needs to tell the other something difficult, let's address the situation without blame.
- Let's try not to sweep issues under the rug.
- Let's try to avoid blurting out our feelings in anger.
- We should feel free to say to each other: I would rather you let me do my dishes. I would rather you help me with the children than the cooking. I would rather help you today, not tomorrow.
- I would like to clean up for you; would that be okay?

How Can We Help Our Child through Her Divorce?

Saul and Lucille were feeling great pain. Their daughter Katie had suddenly told them she and Len, her husband, were getting a divorce. Though Katie called them frequently, she never told them what had happened, nor what was happening. Only the minimum. Saul and Lucille felt left out. Before they learned about the divorce, they had no idea Katie and Len were troubled. They visited a few times a year for a few days, and while the marriage seemed to be missing something in recent visits, they could not name what it was.

And then came the news that Len was moving across the country, leaving Katie. Katie called her parents often but said little about how she felt about this massive change in her life. She seemed to want her parents to fill the silences. Lucille and Saul wanted to know if I had any ideas of how they could be supportive of her daughter. They felt partly responsible, helpless, unsure of what to say or do. They worried about their grandchildren, and about Katie being alone. They wondered about Len, whom they had come to love, about his parents and the other relatives who were no longer part of the family.

I suggested that Lucille tell her daughter that she was open to listening to anything and everything Katie wanted to tell her, and then to follow through by simply listening. She did this, but Katie did not want to talk about her divorce. Katie never did tell her parents much about the reasons for ending her marriage. The divorce was obviously a subject she wanted to keep to herself. But she did remain close to her parents and talked to them a great deal about the children. As for Lucille and Saul, after recognizing Katie's right to avoid talking about her divorce, they found themselves better able to concentrate on their lives.

Jacqueline had an entirely different experience. Lila, her highly successful daughter, had wanted to divorce her husband, but now she was calling her mother daily, crying, asking for help, telling Jacqueline more than she wanted to know. At first Jacqueline was thrilled that Lila was turning to her in her time of need, but soon she began to feel helpless. The conversations were taking a lot of emotional energy and time. How long was this going to go on? Did she have the patience to keep being present for her daughter? Should she be quietly discouraging all this emoting? Should she be more helpful in some unclear way? What was best for her daughter? What was best for her?

Jacqueline did not want to silence or push away Lila, but she did not feel comfortable continuing at this level of intensity. After a few weeks, Jacqueline realized she needed to protect herself a little while still being supportive of her daughter. She began by saying, "I am so sad you are still feeling upset by the divorce. I can't talk as long today. I have to go out in half an hour." And then Jacqueline went on to talk of other things. In another conversation a few weeks later, she asked Lila, "What is going well for you these days?" Jacqueline used this question to bring attention to the fact that good moments are present even in the middle of divorce, and that she wanted to hear about these moments, too.

With such subtle comments, Jacqueline was able to redirect the conversation and feel less at the mercy of Lila's emotions. She also felt the conversations were helping to move Lila on with her life. She was proud that she had found a way to be supportive of her daughter's strengths as well as her struggles.

How Long Should I Give Financial Support?

As children become adults, issues around money tend to arise. Each family needs to determine its own standards and the limits of financial assistance, based on the parents' ability to give and the adult child's need for independence and growth to self-sufficiency.

Some young adults easily accept money, although they may want no strings attached: A gift is a gift. Others will accept money only for certain purposes, or even refuse all help. For everyone to feel comfortable, all family members need to recognize and then communicate their wishes, their needs, and their boundaries. Setting a limit on the time frame and the amount of money is important for the independence of the younger person, and the comfort and duration of the relationship. All parties need to agree from the start and stick to the agreement. A parent needs to feel useful, not used. An adult child needs to feel emotionally supported not dependent and helpless.

Kyle was invited to join a large law firm in New York City after he graduated from law school. He wanted to eliminate his $120,000 in student loans as fast as he could. He wanted to learn how to practice corporate law and then specialize in environmental law. His future looked assured. His family was proud of him. But then the layoffs of 2009 began, and Kyle, a junior staff member, was laid off with two weeks notice. Brooke, his wife, worked as a teacher and had her own student loans. They did not know where to turn. Kyle did not want to ask his parents for help. He knew their retirement funds had been greatly reduced, and he and his father had never talked about money in a forthright manner. He had always found it painful to ask for money, and to receive it when freely given.

Kyle's parents knew he had been laid off and they wanted to help, but they did not want to go into debt. His father, Arthur, was pleased he was in a position to help, but he was always cautious about spending, and he was concerned because he did not know how long his support would be needed. Recognizing that their son was in financial difficulty, one evening Kyle's parents raised the subject during a telephone conversation. They wanted to help. Kyle listened. While he was relieved that his parents had opened the door, he was not ready to accept their help.

Arthur spoke first. This was so unusual that Kyle listened. "I hear you are reluctant to accept our help," said Kyle's father. "I would have difficulty in your place too, but the world has changed and as a father I really want to help you. I think if you had a child who needed help, no matter how old, and you could help, you would step forward and do what you could."

Surprised by what his father said, Kyle felt they might be able to work out something. Kyle had already looked into other jobs, including substitute teaching at his wife's school. When he had done all he could, he reported to his father that he and Brooke had enough to live on but no way to pay off their student loans. Kyle's parents decided to come to New York to visit. Brooke's parents, who also lived out of town, were invited to come, too, because they had also offered to provide financial assistance.

The six of them met around the dining room table in Kyle and Brooke's apartment. Not wanting to make Kyle and Brooke into dependent children, both sets of parents waited for either Kyle or Brooke to take the lead. Kyle spoke. He talked about the situation— their financial needs, their plan to sustain themselves for the present, and their gratitude to their parents for offering to help. Then the parents could speak about their concerns: How much money is needed? For how long? How can we help in a respectful way that allows you to maintain your autonomy and independence?

Together they were able to make a plan. They all felt they had come to a good solution. They would revisit the subject at the end of three months, at which time they would meet again. What worked was the honesty and openness of each of them and the care they took in setting up the conversation. The willingness to help, but not too much, on the part of the parents made a difference. The willingness of the young couple to accept what was difficult to accept allowed for resolution. Kyle let go of the old story that he could not talk about money with his father. His father experienced the joy of giving without fear and caution.

Many families do not have the money to help. Sometimes the older generation or a sibling may need help. People are responding to the economic crisis in many different ways. Kyle always kept in the back of his mind the idea that if the conversation with his parents did not go well, he could hire a mediator, trained in family financial arrangements, to help them formulate a plan. The arrangements are different in each situation, based on the needs of those who have diminished income and the ability and willingness to help by those with more resources. Paying attention to the underlying feelings about giving and receiving is necessary when money is involved.

Conclusion

As new members join a family through the marriage of their adult children, communication changes. Parents need to hold back their opinions and instead ask questions. Adult children need to speak up, with respect. Both generations need to be clear about what they will and won't say and do, and then check on the repercussions of their decisions. As parents pull back, adult children have room to grow and prove themselves as functioning adults and as parents. Both generations are now in a position to enjoy each other's company, spend time together, and enter into a growing friendship of equals.

CHAPTER 9

Repairing a Rift between Parents and an Adult Child

Parents disinherit children. Children dismiss their parents. Some-times they leave home, move far away, do not call, and give a clear message that they do not want their parents calling. How can these breaks in a relationship be bridged? How can understanding be reached? How can forgiveness arise?

What Is Going On When an Adult Child Breaks Off from His or Her Family?

Sometimes young adults find it necessary for their growth and sense of autonomy to separate themselves from their parents and siblings. They do not write, call, or visit. Some move far away. Some stay in the same city but make no contact and give out no addresses or phone numbers. How do parents respond? Some leave messages on answering machines or send e-mails. Others ask friends to tell them if they ever run into the child. One parent I know writes daily to her son. Mostly, parents just wait, hoping to learn sooner or later that the child is well.

Going after an adult child who is obviously trying to put some distance between herself and her family will usually only push her further away. If her parents can bear to do nothing, sooner or later their daughter will wonder what is going on at home and, when she is ready, will call. And while they wait, parents count the days, and they count the ways they went wrong. They may talk about the estrangement to each other and to their friends, sometimes endlessly. Sometimes they keep the pain bottled up and say nothing to anyone. But parents always know when they last saw their child, what was said, how the rift began, and when they last reached out.

When a young adult needs some time out, that need should be respected. Any approach a parent makes feels like a demand. Letting the child initiate contact is usually best. Parents can assure their estranged son that they love him, that they will be available when he wants to return, and that they are willing to talk about what it would take to make the relationship continue. He knows you are there. He knows you will take him back. But after repeatedly being pushed away, his parents can let him know that they are not going to reach out anymore, that he will need to initiate contact. In this way, parents give over the control of the relationship and protect themselves from the repeated experience of being refused or rebuffed.

If the relationship is going to resume, the terms will have to be set by the child. If a grown daughter needs space, stepping into her space and reaching out won't bring her back. Instead, when she is pulling away let her stretch the invisible rope of connection to the distance she needs. When she feels no one holding the other end, only then might she say, "Hey, where are you? How are you? What are you doing?"

Allowing a son to go into the world without being in touch is very difficult, but the way to reconciliation comes from expecting nothing and getting on with life. If his parents have been clear that they love him but are not going to make contact, this response is not heartless. The parents are communicating a solid respect for their own desires and a clear message that contact is up to him. After he returns is the time for conversation—not before.

Opening a conversation about the time apart, which has usually been a painful experience for both the parents and the child, takes courage from both parties. But the conversation can be healing and opens the way to a new relationship. For the child who has left, finding the words to bridge the gap takes courage. Some adult children may just reappear at a family function and act as though nothing needs to be said. An estranged child who has re-entered the family usually needs some time to develop a certain amount of trust that the engagement will be different. Now the parents have to decide how they want to proceed. Is it enough to accept the return of the prodigal child without asking any questions? Some parents may want to admonish, blame, demand, or be unforgiving, but these reactions are likely to prolong the entry into a new, adult relationship.

What Can I Say about My Need for Time Away?

Here are some of the words that young people have used to explain their need to distance themselves from their parents:

- I was developing my own sense of an autonomous self.
- I need to feel less dependent and to prove my self-sufficiency.
- I was not ready to share my joys and sorrows.
- I felt as though my experiences were stolen away from me and made into stories for everyone else.
- I wanted to find my own lifestyle and feel secure in it before discussing it with you.
- I wanted to make my decisions in my own way and time, without interference.
- I needed to recover from the familial sexual abuse and the fact that no one believed me.
- I was tired of being the responsible person, with everyone dependent on me for emotional support.

- I felt I had let you down, and I could never return the huge amount of love you had for me. I was ashamed of who I had become, I could not have you see me as I am now. If you loved me less, it would be easier to bear seeing you.

What Might Parents Ask When They Want to Understand Their Child's Absence?

Here are some things parents might say after their adult child returns and a natural, easy connection has been re-established:

- Having no contact with you was difficult for us.
- We really don't understand what was happening with you at that time.
- We hope you will tell us about your need to be away.
- We will listen and try not to criticize.
- We know your need to have time apart is a hard topic to discuss.
- Please trust us to accept what you say.
- I am sorry that my behavior hurt you.
- I will try not to do that again. I am now ready to talk with you and listen to you without pushing you away or being demanding.
- I missed you.
- I love you.
- I hope we can accept and respect each other from now on.

The parents and their estranged child can now begin to work at developing an adult-to-adult relationship in which they give each other the information and respect that they give their friends. A child who has pulled away does not want to return to an over-interested, possibly engulfing family in which they would again be expected to play a large role. She needs some distance and an appreciation for who she is.

Getting to know our children as adults is the last piece of parenting we do. Treating grown children as we treat very close friends—with love, respect, and acceptance; with attention to their issues and a willingness to negotiate—is the way we might move forward into an adult-to-adult relationship. A conversation opening might sound like this, and either parents or their adult children might be the first to speak:

- Thanks for raising this difficult subject.
- Talking with you about the time you were absent has been good.
- I'd like to make plans to see you again.
- I am so delighted for you.
- I am interested in what you just said.
- I love being with you.
- I love getting to know the person you have become.
- I hope you will keep me up to date about ...

No demands. No judgments. No guilt. No blame. Few or no questions, as questions can feel intrusive. Compliments, true compliments, go a long way toward rebuilding a relationship. Appreciation and gratitude, from the adult child to the parent and vice versa, add to the good will that builds a lasting relationship.

How Can I Reconnect with My Father?

After about a month of therapy I began hearing about Hiram. Claudia was ready to introduce him to her parents. "I know if I go home and tell my father I am going to marry Hiram, no matter what fancy schools he has been to and no matter that his father is a doctor, my dad may never speak to me again. But I have to marry Hiram. I have never been so fully myself, so free to be who I am supposed to be, so happy. I cannot lose this man to my parents' old-country ways. I gave up a previous boyfriend for them and I am not going to do that again. This is my life. Hiram is African-American, and we will have enough to face with his black-pride friends and some of his relatives when they hear he is marrying an Italian."

Claudia decided that first she would go home and tell her parents about Hiram before she introduced them. Her parents had taught Claudia to care about other people, but they also raised her to marry an Italian. She told me that she planned to say: "Mom and Dad, I am in love with the man I want to spend my life with. I want so much for you to meet him. I know you will see past the color of his skin and appreciate what a fine person he is. He is African-American."

When Claudia did speak to her parents, barely pausing for a breath, her father burst out, "You can't bring him home. Not now or ever. This is not your home anymore. Do you understand? You knew not to do this to us. The one thing we ever asked was that you marry an Italian. You have gone too far. I adored you as a baby, as a baby with your black curls and sparkling brown eyes. How could you? Have you no respect? This is no way to behave. No more. I can't look at you without weeping."

"Dad, if you love me so much, then let me be free to marry the man I love," Claudia responded. But her father sat in silence.

"What could I do?" she asked me. "I kissed my mother, who remained silent throughout the exchange. I felt relieved because I had been honest and asked for acceptance, yet at the same time I felt beaten. I had not wanted to have to choose between my family and Hiram. I had always known the importance of Italy to my father, who had kept his old-country ways, but I was hoping to bring him into *this* country. And I wanted to be free of all his rules. He can't stand that. He feels betrayed by me and I feel betrayed by him. I hate to do this but I can't live his way anymore."

Claudia and I discussed how she might want to deal with her parents in the future. She wanted only and adamantly to go on with her life—without her parents. She planned to go ahead with her marriage to Hiram. She had not thought past the wedding. She and Hiram were leaving town soon to start new jobs in Austin, and she felt the timing was good. I asked what her thoughts were about saying goodbye to her parents. She said she was too hurt to consider that. I told Claudia that when she was ready to approach her father, I would help her find the words.

A few years later, when Claudia and Hiram moved back to New York, she and I met for a walk. She brought her two-year-old son to meet me. "He looks a lot like my family and a little like Hiram's," she told me. She also told me that she knew from watching Hiram's mother how much having a grandchild meant. This prompted her to call home one day when she knew her father would be out. She and her mother had a long talk. Then she took the baby to visit her mother, and they spent the afternoon at a nearby playground. "In a way, this suits me," Claudia said. "I don't have to deal with Dad. I am still furious with him for so many things: for making me feel like a useless doll to be adored, for not appreciating me as a person when I was young, for trying to make me in his image, for being so obstinate and cutting me out of his life. So this is how it is."

For several years, Claudia continued with this arrangement. Then Claudia's father became ill. One day when she took her son to see his grandmother, her father was home in bed. Claudia called upstairs. "Don't worry, Dad. We won't bother you." After a while, Claudia's father came downstairs. He pretended that he wanted to make some tea, and he acted as though he saw Claudia everyday. Claudia smiled at him. He smiled back at her.

Claudia was thrilled about the reconciliation, but she wondered what she might have said or done to make it happen earlier. What about all those years she had missed her family? Did they have to wait for illness and age to mellow them? Could Claudia have come home sooner and had this same result? Could the father have admitted his mistake earlier and had years of pleasure with his daughter and her family? Is it so hard to reach out?

What if Claudia had begun calling and asking to talk to her father? What if she had sent baby pictures to both her parents? What if she had a sibling invite them all to dinner? What if she had told her mother she did not like the way things were and asked her to help Claudia reconnect with her father? What if she had come back to her parents' house with Hiram a few weeks after the first stormy encounter and asked her father to meet him before he made up his mind? She might have said, "I know this is really hard for you, but losing you is impossible for me. I need you in my life. Please don't let old rules stand in the way of our love." When her baby was born, she could have said something as simple as:

- I need an Italian grandfather for my child.
- Don't make me choose.
- I want to love Hiram *and* you.
- I'm sorry that my loving Hiram has hurt you so much.
- I'm sorry a misunderstanding has come between us.

Maintaining a break in a relationship is actually more difficult than building a bridge over a rupture. Every day that Claudia and her father were apart, they thought about each other and felt bad. If one of them had picked up the phone and reached out to the other with forgiveness, they might have had contact sooner. Finally, Claudia was the one to reach out, though it could have been the father. So few words are needed:

- I am sorry.
- I want to see you.

These words may not work initially, but they can be repeated until the other responds. The words are small and gentle. The act is one of great courage.

How Can I Reconnect with My Son?

"I need to make peace with my son. I need him at this point in my life. I don't want to die without a relationship, for his sake as well as for my own. I need to reach out to him, but it is so hard." Bill was turning eighty-four. He had retired years before, but was now slowing down. He was now looking around to see who would help him at the end of his life.

Bill had divorced forty years earlier and involved himself in his work as a way of not dealing with the pain of losing his family. "I threw myself into my work, avoiding the whole situation by working more than full time," he told me. Bill's son Jackson lived with his mother after the divorce, which meant that Bill could work late and devote himself completely to his job.

As an adult, Jackson eventually broke contact with his mother as well as his father. Now that Bill was older he had time to think. "I am eighty-four. I don't work. Everything is slow and a little uncomfortable," he told me. "I haven't had any real illness, just the little things that make life harder. I realize that someday I will die. I want to reunite with my son."

Bill wanted to contact Jackson but didn't know how. Should he write to him? What would he say? Where would he begin? Should he apologize? "What can I write to him so he will answer?" he asked me. Bill imagined writing this letter to his son:

Dear Jackson,

It has been too long and I am getting older. I would like to see you and speak with you and get to know you now as an adult in these, my last years. I want to hear from you: What went wrong for you in your life and what has gone well? I would like to tell you about my life and the choices I have made. I would like to have a chance to apologize to you for any hurt I may have caused you. Let us start gently. Happy Birthday, last week. I have been thinking about you and how you were as a small boy.

Love, Bill

After thinking about his son long and hard, Bill decided to send this letter and to sign it with his name, making no claims on the kinship until later. "Let us start out as two adult people," he decided.

Once the letter was mailed, Bill started to worry. Had he set himself up for disappointment? Would Jackson write back? Realizing that writing to Jackson was something he had to do, he also understood that the next step was his son's. This felt uncomfortable, but he had no choice. "I hope he is somewhat past the years of blame and anger," Bill told me. "I hope he has had some success in his life to draw on." As he waited for Jackson to reply, Bill wondered how he had failed to realize sooner that his son would be more important to him in the end than his career, which seemed to mean so much to him during Jackson's childhood.

Jackson did not respond for weeks, and then he wrote that he thought it was too late to undo the past. Bill was heartbroken. He waited awhile and wrote again. Bill worked very hard to write a letter that would express his desire and at the same time not demand anything of Jackson.

Dear Jackson,

I am here. I don't think it is too late. I am alive, and I want to connect to you. I am very different from how I was when we last met. I suspect you are too. I am interested in talking with you.

Love, Bill.

Bill hoped Jackson would respond, but in the meantime, saying what was on his mind and in his heart helped him feel better. He realized that he couldn't force a relationship or even a response from his son. He had to wait until his son was ready.

For the next two years, Bill wrote to Jackson several times a year. Finally, he received a Christmas card. Then a birthday card came with a short note. Bill became hopeful. He sent Jackson his e-mail address and they began to correspond. After they had sent many casual notes back and forth, Jackson asked Bill to tell him his side of the divorce. In his response Bill tried to be as objective as possible, without blaming his ex-wife or putting himself down. He did not want to make Jackson feel in any way at fault.

At the moment, Bill is still waiting for a visit with Jackson. He has become calm and more content about the relationship. He knows that when they get together, he may need to again go over his side of the divorce story. He is prepared to apologize for his treatment of Jackson, especially during the time of the divorce. Bill looks forward to hearing from Jackson about how his life has unfolded. He wants to enter gently into the relationship. He knows Jackson may be angry, and he wants to stay calm and just listen.

If they do get together, Bill may need to jump-start the conversation by talking about something neutral, making no claims on his son. He might have to acknowledge that the moment is difficult and suggest a superficial topic to get them talking: "I'm sure you're nervous, and I know I am. I am interested in simple things, such as what you did yesterday. I want to know about your life." Or they might simply take a walk, not talking much at all. This will be the beginning; the door may be open.

How Can I Get My Whole Family Together Again?

Steph made it clear she wanted nothing to do with her family. She had lived at home with her mother and two aunts until age twenty-five. Her older brothers lived out of state. Her mother tried to respect her daughter's need for time alone, but she continued to send checks and cards for birthdays and holidays. Steph felt these were strings binding her. She pulled farther away. She sent back angry notes. She did not stay in touch with her brothers. Steph's mother finally understood that Steph truly needed distance. She decided that she would no longer send cards, money, or gifts. Steph's distancing, her not even saying "thank you" for her gifts, helped her mother realize she had to cut the cord and wait for Steph to reach out to her.

After ten years of this estrangement, one of the older brothers initiated family therapy and invited Steph to come. She accepted the invitation. During the first therapy session, Steph explained her problem with the family and how hurt she had been. As the youngest, she felt they had treated her as a child for far too long. They expected her to be their pet, not their equal. She felt misunderstood and unappreciated for her interests and talents. Ten years ago she had not even wanted to try communicating with them. She had needed to become strong herself in order to take them on. Both brothers told Steph how much they missed her and how hurt they were by her seeming disregard for the family, especially for their mother.

In a subsequent session the therapist moved the conversation on to what each family member wanted in his or her future relationship with each other. He helped them speak with respect and listen quietly, trying to hear each other's point of view. Steph said she wanted to be part of the family again. She wanted to be invited to family events and holidays. She wanted to get to know her nieces. She said that despite their original disdain for her plan to pursue acting, she had moved ahead in that field and was willing to live from job to job in order to do what she loved. She hoped they would come and see her in a play. She told them her stage name.

They had no idea she had appeared in plays they might have actually gone to see. Steph gave them her address, cell phone number, and home number. She said she wanted to introduce them to her fiancé.

The family was amazed. Little Stephie had grown up—and without their expertise and training. They could easily respect this new, clearly adult person, and to congratulate her for her successes. They wanted to include her in family events. They were excited about seeing her act.

Steph was not sure how interpret this new way of being treated. She felt herself being pulled back into feeling less than she was. She sat quietly through one entire session, and when asked by the therapist what was going on, she said she was having trouble maintaining a sense of herself, of remaining polite and being engaged. She wanted to be accepted just as a person, not because she was successful in her career or entering a marriage that met with her family's approval. She wanted them to like her for herself, but she did not know how to get that across.

The therapist encouraged the family to make plans to get together in pairs, separate from the large family gatherings, so each person could get to know Steph and she could get to know them. They all realized that feeling like a family again would take time, but the effort was worthwhile.

What Will We Talk About When We Meet?

Andrew was just starting out in life. He was the only child of a single mother, Florence, who thought the world of him. He did not know if he could live up to all her expectations. He needed to be on his own in the world without trying to please her every step of the way. He needed areas of privacy in his life and did not want to tell her everything that happened to him, whether good or bad.

When he was in his twenties he told her that he was not going to see her for a while. Andrew told his mother that he loved her, that he would not be gone forever, but he needed some time alone.

Florence did not believe him. Every day, every holiday, every birthday seemed like ten years. Their lives had been easy; they were not used to pain and loss and nonacceptance from loved ones. She couldn't resist phoning him. He took her calls but repeatedly told her he would not talk about certain things. She wanted to visit. He said no. She invited him home. He said no.

Three years went by. Finally, worn out by the superficial quality of the phone calls, Florence stopped calling. Months went by and Andrew did not call his mother. Then, when Florence e-mailed him that she was coming to his city for a conference and wanted to see him, he said, "Yes, I am ready." Her heart lifted.

Florence decided ahead of time not to ask any questions. Conversations with Andrew early in the three-year separation, and Florence's conversations with her friends to try to understand, helped her realize that he had wanted some privacy. He wanted a sense that his world belonged to him, not to her. Florence understood that her questions could feel intrusive, that any question takes the conversation where the person asking wants it to go, and that using questions could feel like pressure. She decided that when she saw Andrew, she would let him talk about what he wanted to, and she, in turn, would speak of things that were of interest to both of them. No questions.

They talked of music and art, plays, movies and books, even the weather. At one point, Florence asked Andrew if the weather was going to be nice the next day and then kicked herself under the table. (That was a question.) They had a constricted but cautiously good time. At the end of their visit, he said, "Can I see you tomorrow?" Florence began breathing fully for the first time in three years. That night she slept well.

For this family, the rupture was being repaired. Florence learned the value of not asking questions, of just being present for what her child wanted to tell her. She wanted Andrew to be assured of her interest without feeling engulfed. When she did not ask any questions, when she listened with attention and respect, she learned what she needed to learn and her son felt safe in the circle of her love.

Conclusion

The relationship between parents and adult children is in constant flux. Each person is constantly growing and changing. Since so much is at stake, family relationships need a great deal of attention, respect, and care. After an adult child breaks away and is absent for a long period of time, which may have seemed easier than staying to work things out, even more care needs to be taken to achieve rapprochement.

CHAPTER 10

Supporting Adult Children as They Become Parents

A baby arrives in the world, and is passed around and hugged by family members of all the generations. When each of my grandchildren arrived, my heart expanded and my eyes filled with tears of joy. Another person to love had arrived on the planet. My husband and I were excited by each small bundle of human life that came into our lives.

My first grandchild arrived when I was fifty-six. Because I had studied child development and I had raised three children, I thought my children would be delighted to have my expertise. I had so many ideas on how to correctly raise children. Why would they want to start from scratch when here I was a fount of knowledge?

For four years I facilitated groups for mothers of very young children, with endless talk about toilet training, sleep patterns, marital relationships, and how to live in the world as a new mother. I wanted to give all that, plus all my academic learning and what I had learned from my own mothering, to my children and grandchildren. I knew not to pile on the expertise, but to let them find their way. I knew the importance of respecting the parents' style and wishes. I knew to wait until they asked for my input. Yet when my first grandchild arrived, I heard hundreds of opinions spilling out of my mouth. My grandson was dressed too warmly, he should not be sleeping in the car, he should always be burped for five minutes after feeding. I always had a better idea.

My husband and I lived on the East Coast at the time. All our children were living on the West Coast. We visited every three or four months and then returned home. Since our children did not need to deal with us often, they just politely listened to my advice and continued to do what worked for them and their baby. When the baby was about eighteen months old and would obviously survive without my input, and survive well, I relaxed and let go. I wish I had let go at the start. Children really need to be the parents. As a grandmother, my role now is only to give fully accepting love to my grandchildren and to support and encourage their parents. The first grandchild, and then two more, grew more and more delightful, expressive, funny, and original. They were good company, healthy, sociable, safe, and loved.

I remember too well my own mother-in-law doubting my ability to adequately breast-feed my new baby, to calm her, or to determine her proper nap time. I wished my mother-in-law would notice what an amazing job I was doing only three weeks after the baby was born. I wished she had let me know that caring for a newborn is a difficult job and that every mother doubts she is getting it right. I wish she had supported and praised me for what I was able to accomplish. As a grandmother, I remembered to say such things to my children. My husband and I have given sincere and accurate compliments to the new parents in our family, knowing how tentative most of us feel as new parents and how much we want to hear that we are doing well.

Who Gets to Name the Baby?

Brenda and Ron loved the name conversations they had during Brenda's pregnancy. They liked the names they had chosen, including a middle name for Brenda's maternal grandmother. But Joyce, Ron's mother, did not like that name. In her family, the name had brought bad luck, and even Brenda's maternal grandmother had died when her three children were still very young. In the hospital the day the birth certificate was to be signed, Joyce decided to intervene in the naming decision. "I don't want to make a fuss," she said, "and I don't want to hurt your feelings, Brenda. I know the names you have chosen please you and are really your business. But I would like you to find any other name; that would mean a lot to me. This name scares me, but I understand that the final decision is up to you." Then she told them she would leave them alone to discuss the subject.

Brenda and Ron talked. "Should we give in to Mother? Was she asking too much? What was this bad luck idea?" This was a difficult situation. They had not expected Ron's mother to be so superstitious. They decided to make a slight change in the baby's middle name so they were able to please themselves and their mother.

Ron and Brenda were able to come to such an agreeable decision because of the way Ron's mother had made her suggestion. She let them know she respected them and, at the same time, she explained her own desires. Then she left them alone to talk about their decision. Her way of handling the situation made them want to please her.

How Do I Respond to My Children's Questions?

When my children do occasionally ask for my opinion, I feel very appreciated. Yet I am not as easy and flowing with my words as I wish to be. I do such a good job with the conversation in my head, but during the delivery I tend to preach and I don't listen well. I have learned to come back the next day and apologize for whatever I later realize needs to be rewritten.

Here are some of the things I say when I am at my best:

- What are you thinking of doing about this issue?
- How do you think that will work out?
- What are your concerns?
- Here is what I think you might try.
- Have I said too much?
- Do you want more?

My husband and I love our grandchildren so much, and we want only for them to grow up confident, loving, and curious. My part as a grandmother requires wisdom and compassion—the wisdom to know my children's job is to shape their children and the compassion to remember what a hard job that can be. I need to be present, accepting, supportive, and loving. At times I need to act with restraint and control my desire to be an expert. I speak up only when necessary for the welfare of the child, and always in a way that respects the parents.

Is It Okay to Speak Up for Health?

Marilyn lived in rural Maine and had decided not to inoculate her children. She felt vaccinations were unnecessary in today's world, when so many diseases have been eradicated. She had read articles that suggested inoculation was not risk free, that vaccinations for infants might play a role in the development of autism. The more she learned, the more she did not want to expose her children to the risks of these unnecessary procedures. After all, if the other children were inoculated, how would her children be exposed?

Lynn, Marilyn's mother, was not happy with this decision and couldn't stop thinking about how vulnerable her grandchildren would be without their vaccinations. Finally, she realized she had to say something. She waited until she was with her daughter. Then she calmly said: "I see what good care you take of your children.

SUPPORTING ADULT CHILDREN AS THEY BECOME PARENTS

I see you trying very hard to be the best mother possible. I know you think things through before making a decision. Yet I find I disagree with you on only one point. I am going to say this once and only once, and I hope you will consider what I am saying. This is not my business, but I think having your children inoculated is very important."

Marilyn did change her mind, but not for a few years. When she told her mother that she'd had the children inoculated, Lynn patted herself on the back for not repeating her opinion and for not making the inoculations into an issue between them. By being respectful of her daughter's right to make decisions for her children, Lynn was able to speak her mind and maintain the relationship with her daughter, which was as important to her as her grandchildren's health.

Is It Okay to Speak Up for Safety?

Sally loved her two granddaughters. Being with them was such a sweet encounter. She felt her heart overflowing with love each time they entered her home, and each time the instant she touched the knocker they opened the door for her when she arrived at their apartment in New York City. Camellia, Sally's daughter, loved being able to ask Sally to babysit for an hour while she ran errands, child free. Sally loved time alone with the children, especially when they were learning to talk. Sally was aware that as she'd grown older, she had become more anxious, and when she took her grandchildren out into the world, she was very conscious not to pass on her irrational anxieties.

When the children were three and five years old, the family moved to an apartment that was not much farther away but it had a balcony. Camellia and her husband Tom loved the balcony; they had been longing to open a door and step out to see what the day was like, without having to go into the hall and down an elevator. The grandchildren, too, were very excited about the move. The old building was beautiful, but when Sally took one look at the balcony railing, all the air went out of her chest. Instead of saying anything, she closed her lips and thought about her dilemma. Should she spoil her children's joy and act parental and overly protective, or should she risk the lives of her darling grandchildren? Which is more important, she asked herself: her relationship with her daughter or her grandchildren's safety? Camellia could see her mother biting her tongue. She did not know why, but she knew that look. She had seen it as a girl. She could not imagine what was going on in her mother's mind, and she was not going to pay any attention.

One day Sally ran into Tom's mother on the elevator. They quickly ascertained that they had similar qualms about the balcony, and they decided that together they would approach Camellia and Tom and quietly tell them what they were thinking: "We would like to talk to you about something. You are very conscientious parents and we don't want to make you feel you did anything wrong. If we are out of line, please tell us. We think the railing on your balcony is not a safe height for the children. Perhaps you are already aware of this and are arranging for a new railing."

Camellia and Tom were surprised. They looked at each other and then at their mothers. They did not want to admit their carelessness. They said they would talk about the safety of the railing and decide what to do. They thanked the women for their advice. Camellia in particular felt frightened for the children and embarrassed that she had not noticed the height of the railing as a problem. She told herself that maybe she had not noticed the railing because the children were still small, but they were growing fast.

When she and Tom talked, she admitted that the mothers were correct. Camellia was then able to tell both of the grandmothers that she would immediately take care of replacing the railing. She expressed her appreciation for both grandmothers' concern for the safety of the children. She also thanked them for being so supportive and nonintrusive during their move into their apartment with the balcony.

By giving their children the benefit of the doubt rather than accusing them of neglect, the two grandmothers created space for Camellia and Tom to make an appropriate decision regarding the safety of the grandchildren. The building superintendent arrived two days later with the supplies to build the requested three-foot railing around the balcony. Tom and Camellia got their fresh air, and the girls could go out on the balcony and stand on their tiptoes to look at the buildings across the street. The grandmothers and the parents sighed with relief.

How Can I Choose between a Child and a Grandchild?

Reggie often corrected his four-year-old son Ben. He wanted his son's grammar and pronunciation to be perfect. He wanted his manners to be perfect. Grandpa Douglas watched and grimaced. He had been corrected a lot during his childhood; with his children, he had tried not to repeat that behavior. He wanted to protect his grandson, yet he did not want to make his son feel wrong. As a long-time educator, Douglas knew that the young boy's sense of self was at stake, and he felt he had an obligation to say something. Douglas had to balance concern for his son's pride in his fathering with his grandson's need for protection, while trying to maintain a positive relationship with both of them. Douglas found himself in a difficult place.

One evening when his grandson was asleep, Douglas opened the subject with Reggie: "I love the way you play with Ben and engage him in conversation. You take a real interest in him. Your patience is lovely to watch. Your love for him shines through. But I want to talk to you about something. I want to do this in a helpful way. I don't want to hurt you or Ben. And I don't want you to feel watched by me. Where I am coming from is my own experience as a child. My father and mother were always telling me I hadn't talked right, walked right, run right, played the game right, done my homework right, made my bed right. You aren't as constant in your corrections as my parents were, but often I do hear you speak to Ben about the way he says things. I feel protective of Ben when you do that. I tried so hard not to do that to you."

Reggie sat silently, looking as he had as a teenager. His head was down, his face expressionless.

Douglas then asked him, "Have I been too heavy with you? I am sorry if I have. I don't like to correct you any more than I like to hear you correct Ben. How are my comments sitting with you?"

Reggie thought for a while. He knew his father was trying to reach him, but he had wanted to appear to be the very best of fathers in front of his father. To do so, he realized, he had tried too hard—and at the expense of Ben. He was not as hard on Ben when Douglas was not around. He began to speak these thoughts out loud. Douglas was so relieved to hear his son speak in a thoughtful way that he went over and hugged Reggie. Enough had been said. Reggie had the opportunity to save face; Douglas had the opportunity to express his concerns; and Ben was protected from his father's expectations of him.

How Can I Help?

Learning to be a grandparent does not happen the instant the first grandchild is born. Only with time do grandparents learn that the ease of loving a grandchild comes with the consciousness that the mother and father of the baby are going to do things their way. We must remind ourselves to be especially careful about the middle generation as our hearts open to the new, small, do-no-wrong beings.

As a new grandmother, Sarah thought about how she could be helpful without undermining Cindy, her daughter-in-law. For the first few weeks after her birth, Elizabeth did not breast-feed easily. When the baby cried, and Cindy became nervous and anxious, Sarah watched and wondered: Should she intervene on behalf of the baby and give her a bottle? Or should she be careful of her relationship with her daughter-in-law and let Cindy work it out her way? Sarah found being around the house to be difficult, hearing the baby cry and Cindy worrying out loud. Sarah wanted to hold and comfort the baby, yet she knew she had to let Cindy find her way. Finally Sarah decided to encourage Cindy to seek some help from La Leche League. She also said the following things to Cindy at various times during the course of several days:

- I see you trying to make everything work.
- Caring for a newborn—learning to "read" your child—is difficult.
- I felt inadequate at times when I had a newborn.
- I think you are doing everything possible to give the baby what she needs.
- What a loving, patient mother you are.
- Remaining calm and patient when a baby cries is very difficult.
- I am here. Let's get through this together.
- Is there anything I can do to help you through the most difficult moments?
- Would you like me to rock the baby for a while?
- Shall I make you a cup of tea?

With the words spoken, Sarah backed off, respecting Cindy's sensitivity as a first-time mother. Sarah found jobs in other corners of the house to give Cindy the space to reflect. Realizing that she and

Cindy were sharing the same concerns, Sarah intentionally changed her identity from expert to support person. Having been the mother of a newborn herself, this grandmother realized that what a new mother needs most is to feel she is doing the best job possible.

Four days later the baby easily took to the breast. For Sarah, these were four days of trying hard not to take over. Sarah calmed down, the baby started filling out, and Cindy became a proud, competent mother.

Anthea, another grandmother, did not handle a similar situation so well. Each time the baby seemed hungry, Anthea rushed into the bedroom and started giving advice to her daughter Renata. Sit up higher, pinch your breast more, stroke the baby's cheek. Anthea could not contain her anxiety. She would bark her orders and then tell her daughter, "Relax, just relax." The more Renata was told to relax, the tighter she held her body, shoulders hunched, back bent over. Anthea suggested offering the baby a bottle, a pacifier, a bottle of water. She and Renata quickly became frustrated with each other and the baby.

Anthea did not notice that when she told Renata to relax, she scowled and pulled into herself more tightly. Anthea should have backed off. When calmer, she could have talked about her own difficulties with nursing Renata just after birth: "I am sorry I am so anxious. I was very nervous after you were born. I wanted to make breast-feeding easier for you than it was for me, and I am afraid I am making it worse. I am sorry."

How Can Grandparents Find Ways to Help, Not Hinder?

Martine could not get used to the fact that all her children and their spouses worked outside the home. She was very grateful that when her children were young, she was able stay home with them.

She had waited to go back to work until the last child entered kindergarten, and even then she only worked part time at the school library. None of her children had that luxury; they all had to work. Martine had a hard time understanding all the arrangements they had to make for child care.

Only one of Martine's children, her daughter Olivia, lived near her. Martine's two-year-old grandchild was in a wonderful day-care program. Martine saw how worn out Olivia and her husband were at the end of the day. Getting dinner on the table, having a little playtime, and getting the three children (ages two, five, and seven) to bed was difficult to handle. Martine, who was retired, decided that she would like to pick up the three children two afternoons a week, which would involve a short car trip to two different schools. She could take them to their home, make them an afternoon snack, spend some time with them, and begin to prepare dinner.

Martine did not want to make the young couple feel they were not taking good care of their children. She did not want to undermine their sense of competence, so when she offered her time, she spoke to them of her desire to spend more time with the children. Often Martine's husband came with her. The young couple was thrilled. Martine and her husband were thrilled. As the plan was implemented, the grandparents loved having this quiet time with their grandchildren. They found in themselves a patience they had never had with their own children. The grandchildren became comfortable with the grandparents, cuddling while reading and even helping with dinner.

Can Grandparents Write Different Rules for Their House?

Emma often brought her grandchildren to her house to play. She realized the value of following the lead of her adult children regarding

rules and rituals: bedtime, bathtime, different areas for noisy play
and quiet play, even how to deal with questionable behavior. She
wanted to follow the parents' routine even at her home. However,
Emma did not agree with Katherine, her daughter, in one area. The
children were used to eating when hungry and walking around with
their food. Emma wanted food to be eaten at the kitchen table, at
defined mealtimes, with one afternoon snack. She did not want to
be popping in and out of the kitchen all day, preparing food, cleaning up crumbs all over the house, and doing dishes. She wanted to
be supportive of Katherine, but in her house Emma also wanted to
handle food her way. She needed to speak to her daughter about
what to do.

When she spoke to her daughter Emma said: "I love being with
your children. I completely respect and agree with all the ways you
want me to interact with them. I have only one area of difference
I want to talk to you about. When the children are at my house, I
would like to feed them three meals a day, plus an afternoon snack,
and have them eat at the kitchen table. Do you think they can handle that? Can you allow that?"

Katherine grimaced but then agreed that the children could have
more structured meals at Emma's house. She also gave Grandma
Emma some tips on easy snacks that don't mess up the house or
require dishes: power bars, cheese sticks, Jell-O in small containers.
Emma and Katherine worked out their personal preferences without confrontation or making each other wrong. Each was respectful and appreciative of the other.

How Can Grandparents Talk about Their Needs?

As Mel and Mary approached their mid-seventies, having their
grandchildren visit became more difficult. Their daughter Fran and
the grandchildren came from France for six weeks every summer,

and everything the children said had to be translated. Mary found the service part of her role very taxing, plus they had planned outings every day. The noise level was very high and the energy of the children was at times overwhelming. At the end of the six weeks, Mary always felt exhausted and as if she herself needed a vacation. Mary decided to speak to Fran about her difficulty coping with the long visits. She did not want to offend her daughter, but Mary felt that Fran used the six weeks as a kind of respite from the job of motherhood. Mary found being straight with her daughter to be difficult. She had always taken care of everyone while making it look easy. With apparent ease she had juggled children and a job and Mel and a social life. But now she was less energetic and her ankles hurt all the time. She wanted to see her daughter every summer, but she knew something had to change.

Mary and Mel began planning what to say to Fran. They wanted to engage her in planning the next visit, not just dump their frustration on her. They wanted to include some words of love, along with questions about the length of the stay. Mary said: "Fran, I love you, I love your visits, and I love the children—but your father and I want to talk to you. We are getting older. We need to plan your next visit so we have a good time together in a way that does not leave us worn out at the end. Would you consider staying part of the time with your sister? We love going on expeditions with all of you, but we need to be reminded to stay home and rest while you go out for part of the day. We would like to plan with you ways to simplify mealtime, cooking, and shopping. We love having you here. We want you to come. We just need you to help with the chores."

Hearing these words helped Fran realize that her mother was no longer young. She began doing more of the daily chores when she and the children stayed with her parents. She arranged for shorter visits. Mary and Mel now look forward to the visits and, as a result, the relationship between the grandchildren and grandparents has become richer and more relaxed. Mary was glad she spoke up and sorry she had not done so a few years earlier. She was pleased with herself for engaging with Fran in a way that made Fran a participant in the planning.

How Can I Make Relocating Nearer to My Children and Grandchildren Work for All of Us?

Some people in their sixties and seventies choose to move long distances to be closer to their children and grandchildren. My husband Charlie and I did this. At ages sixty and sixty-one, after living on the East Coast all our lives, we moved to Berkeley, California. Our decision to move began with an explicit invitation from Phil, our middle child. Phil said, "You should move out here and watch our two babies grow up from nearby." Though many people think of doing this on their own, an invitation from Phil and his wife Mary made us seriously consider the idea of moving. Did this mean Phil and Mary were ready for us to live closer than three thousand miles?

At the time, Charlie and I were living in a Manhattan high-rise. Our son Bob was in Portland, Oregon, with his wife Tammy and a child on the way. Our two older children were living in Berkeley—Phil, married with two children, and Ruth, who was planning to marry Marc. We loved our adult life in Manhattan—the rush, the excitement, our friends, and the accessibility of art, theater, and special events. We could easily get on a plane to visit our children as we pleased. In many ways, this suited us very well.

However, the thought of living near our children and their babies was enough to override all the enticements of Manhattan. We began to think about a very appealing way of visiting: popping in and out for a few hours, picking up the grandchildren on a weekend for half a day, the chance to be with my adult children and their spouses one or two at a time instead of all of us for a whole weekend. We began to envision a better way of having relationships with our children and our grandchildren.

Before we put our Manhattan apartment on the market, we needed clarity with all our children. We started out by saying: "We are thinking seriously about moving to Berkeley. We want you to think about how that sits with you. You don't have to answer now, but get back to us with your thoughts, reactions, and fears. Our pleasure would be getting to know you as adults and being more involved with the children than a visit four times a year for four days. Our fears are that we would not have time for our own life and you might feel intruded upon. We need to be able to talk about all these issues, now and from time to time after we move."

Now all our children became involved in the discussion, telling us they thought our contemplated move to the Bay Area would be great. They also agreed that having conversations from time to time would be important—to check in on how our new way of relating was going and to fine-tune the contacts. We agreed that we would all have the right to say, "This is not a good time for a visit." We reassured our children that they could always ask us to help with child care, understanding that we could always say "no" when the timing wasn't good.

To move to a place Charlie and I did not like or a place where we knew no one but the children would not have been an option, but we knew many people in the San Francisco Bay Area, and we loved the natural beauty of the place. After three years of discussing the pros and cons of relocating, we resigned from our jobs, sold our apartment, and moved into a rental house in Berkeley.

Once we arrived, we had further conversations with our children. "When we step on your toes or get out of line in some way, please let us know. We have to work on making this work, and work well. If we are going to live nearby, we have to learn to be very straight and open with each other. We don't know about your day-to-day lifestyle and how to fit into it. Please help us." Our children and their families learned to let us know when we were asking too much or when we hurt their feelings. We tried to be considerate and so did they. Now our children occasionally note that we are away a lot. Sometimes they ask for our help when we are busy. We like to go on outings with our grandchildren when they were not too busy with parties or soccer.

The last time I checked, our children said they were delighted we had moved to Berkeley. That was a great relief. I needed to ask about once a year for the first few years, and then less often to keep the lines of communication flowing and loving. Assessing when someone is carrying hurt feelings may be more difficult. Fears that the experience is not as good as imagined for the people involved need to be addressed, not avoided. Voicing a criticism of even one of our interactions takes courage for any of the three generations. I always like to offer an opening for conversation. For Charlie and me, the connections and intimacy that are the result of our move have enriched our lives immeasurably.

What Should I Do If My Children Do Not Invite Me to Relocate?

For some parents whose children live in other parts of the country, the invitation to move does not come. How do you ask whether your children want to have you nearby? How do you ensure a straight answer? Listening carefully to their words—or being aware if a response to the idea is absent—can reveal a clue that something needs to be discussed.

When parents get no response or an unenthusiastic response, they might say:

- I hear that you are not quite ready for this.
- It sounds like we should wait until it is a good fit for all of us.

- We would like to be near you.
- If we move near you, we do not want you to be the only interest in our life.
- We would want to talk about how to live close to each other without intruding.
- I hope we can explore this possibility again in the future.
- Know that we love you and are interested in your comfort.
- We will ask you again in a few years, and we hope you will open the subject again too, when it feels useful to you.

People should not have to ask permission of their children, but making a decision to relocate needs to include an open conversation among equals about the hopes and intentions of all involved. When everyone has an acceptable level of understanding, plans to relocate can begin to move forward. Tolerance for different ways of doing things, and the ability to let go, love, and accept carry the day.

Conclusion

The relationship between generations is enhanced and becomes more complicated as new generations appear. With openness, sensitivity, and respect, conversations pave the way to a positive outcome. Silence and the harboring of discontent lead nowhere. Recognition of moments of difference and finding the words to discuss them will bring a family together in love and delight. Small children see and hear adults talking about their feelings, the good and the bad, and learn from this.

Grandparents have the opportunity to see their own children as parents and to watch another generation grow up. They are able to offer support and compliments, giving their adult children another round of affirmation and confidence to fulfill their role as parents. The older generation's ability to respect the wishes of their adult children and the middle generation's willingness to appreciate the interests of their parents will keep the river of love flowing through their lives, bringing health and well-being to all.

CHAPTER 11

Nurturing and Reviving Friendships among Siblings

Sibling relationships can be important and nourishing, and they can be conflicted and distant. They can move back and forth between these states many times. Siblings may become so different from each other that finding out they grew up in the same household is hard to believe. Having a shared childhood does not mean that siblings will share values and interests. Even when siblings are getting along, they may be faced with charged conversations. They often bring their past history and the intensity of their relationship to what seems to be a new issue but may have ancient roots. Some siblings find that certain topics are taboo or even stop talking to each other for varying periods of time. Others are best friends and have an easy, flowing, and accepting relationship.

Even when they are close and have much in common, siblings may disagree about child rearing, politics, religion, or lifestyle. Family secrets may be known to one and not to another. Sometimes issues around gender identity and gender preference are swept under the carpet. Ignoring these differences freezes the relationship at a superficial level; day-to-day issues and family gossip replace truth and openness. The time may come to consider having more honest conversations, especially if one person wants to change this uneasy peace. Coming from a place of respect, with a clear intention to enhance the relationship—not to divide and conquer—can cut through the fear and silence and open family members to the truth of each other's lives. The purpose of such a conversation would not be to initiate change but to uncover beliefs we think we know and now want to understand.

Having a relationship of warmth and acceptance, openness and appreciation takes attention. Remembering that the relationship matters more than the differences can help lead to a more open exchange. Neutral subjects are safe, but when political or religious differences come up, or when siblings have radically different economic circumstances, tensions may arise.

What Should I Say When I Disagree with My Sibling's Politics?

Politics can divide siblings, especially during election years, when differences can become crystallized. Siblings should not criticize or attempt to change the mind of each other. Respect and tolerance are required. You are going to be in a relationship for a long time, so the priority is retaining the relationship rather than winning your sibling's vote. On election day one brother, knowing that his sister voted differently from him, said to her, most generously, "I wish your side luck in the election. May the best candidate win." And that was all.

In another family two sisters at opposite ends of the political spectrum carefully avoided the subject of the upcoming election. But one night their husbands, each one aligned with his wife, began to argue. One sister said, "I don't think there is any point going into that subject," and the topic was dropped. But the other sister's husband was not comfortable with the pretense of "getting along." At their next meeting, he proposed that they talk about their differing political views, not with the desire to change each other but rather to appreciate the other couple's views. First he said, "My intention is to maintain a calm, curious, accepting stance. I want to have the conversation in a way that will enhance our relationship, not jeopardize it." Then, in a neutral tone he asked, "How did you come to this point of view?"

Here are other questions that arose in the course of the conversation:

- How does your party loyalty play out in your life?
- How do you feel when you are with us, who think so differently?
- What has kept you from talking about your differences with us?
- How can we support you and yet maintain our own stance?

Each of the four listened politely to the other, with very little cross talk. They made comments about ideas they had not thought of or that made sense to them, but nobody said anything in direct disagreement or with disparagement. Everyone remained calm and rational, discussing what appealed to each about the party or politician of their choice. By reminding themselves this conversation was just to help understand different points of view, they were able to appreciate the other without changing their own position. And they understood better how two sisters had arrived at their different ideas.

How were these two sisters and their husbands able to speak about a difficult, divisive subject that they had been avoiding for years? They started things off with a neutral question. They clearly set the intention to talk calmly and to make sure the relationships did not suffer. They ended by commenting on what was new for each person.

How Can I Reach Out to a Sibling?

Kate was going home for Christmas. Although she was looking forward to being with her family, part of her was dreading another encounter with her sister Maggie. Maggie was older, but Kate felt she had long since achieved enough experience in her life to quit competing with her sister. Yet in Maggie's presence, Kate felt resentment, envy, anger, and judgment coming toward her. She was not looking forward to fending off all this negativity. She also did not want to react as she had in the past, becoming defensive and pulling away.

Before her Christmas trip, Kate began to reflect on what she wanted in her relationship with Maggie. She wanted to cut through the usual games and wondered what she could say to her sister with love, instead of distance. She began to see how she contributed to the division between them. In the past, as soon as she entered the family home she was listening for all the ways Maggie would put her down, judge her, and make her wrong. She would begin the visit feeling distrustful, which made moving toward Maggie more difficult than moving away.

Kate decided she needed to initiate a change in her attitude by saying something positive to Maggie. But what? She was not ready to say "I love you," but she must be able to think of something to say so she and Maggie would be aligned instead of antagonistic. Kate decided to start small. Instead of waiting for the expected confrontation, she would compliment her sister, sincerely, whenever she could.

On arrival, Kate told Maggie that she liked her new hairstyle. Later in the day, she thanked her for doing more than her share of the dishes. All day she lay in wait for good things instead of bad. She focused on finding positive actions, not negative ones. She assumed the best not the worst, so when Maggie said something about Kate always staying up late, Kate did not hear it as a criticism of her unruly life, just a statement. Kate was able to laugh and say, "Yes, my days and nights are a little confused. You are right about that." After a day of this, Kate began to notice a change. Maggie stopped looking for ways to put down Kate. Kate began to feel better about herself in Maggie's presence. Maggie began to compliment Kate. When Kate left, she had less dread of her next meeting with Maggie and was rather pleased with herself.

Kate chose not to initiate a conversation that might have led to resentments and recriminations. Instead, she shifted the relationship with just a few well-placed sincere compliments, some light remarks, and a change of attitude.

How Can I Reach Out to a Sibling I No Longer Know?

As children Claire and her older brother Kent shared a room, a house, parents, and a live-in grandma. They went to the same schools, had the same teachers (who knew they were related), and went to the same Sunday school and summer camp. They shared friends, social events, and gossip. Claire thought that Kent had life all figured out, and the way he lived was a model for her. He married and left town. She, too, married and went to another city. Both were quite successful, she as a lawyer, he as an accountant, and they met less and less often. Claire's good feelings for her brother did not wane. She frequently called him. Kent did not seem to call her much, but, she told herself, keeping relationships alive is a woman's job. She wanted her children to meet their uncle, but she never quite had enough money to visit both her mother in Wisconsin and her brother in Colorado.

After not seeing each other for several years, Claire and Kent both attended their cousin's wedding. Claire found herself working at conversation, and Kent did not seem to notice or to care. She wanted to shake him. The weekend was short, and on the plane home she realized that the many wonderful moments of the weekend did not include her time with Kent. If she wanted to renew her relationship with Kent, Claire decided she would have to do the writing and calling, at least at the start. Somewhat shyly, she called: "I want to be in better touch with you," she began. "I realize we only see each other at family events. I want to catch up with you, your life, and your family. What is a good time for me to call? Would you rather I use e-mail? Are you angry with me for anything? I am hoping you want to reconnect too."

Having taken the first step and received a pleasant response from Kent, Claire went ahead and wrote him a letter, filling him in on aspects of her life and asking about his life. He responded a long time later by e-mail. She did not rush to reply, but she did know that if she did not keep up the effort, he was not going to be the one to jump in. After about a year of somewhat more contact, Claire invited Kent and his family to visit her family. This move toward a full relationship required effort on the part of one sibling. Because of Claire, they were they able to reconnect and open new possibilities.

How Can I Get Along with My Sister-in-Law?

Sister-in-law relationships can become tangled by words that remain unexpressed. If discomfort or desires remain unspoken, neither woman will know what the other is thinking.

Sunny liked being with her family for Thanksgiving. One year, when the dinner was to be held at her brother's house and she was staying with her mother, Sunny sprained her ankle while getting off the plane. Not wanting her mother to worry, she bore the pain in silence. On Thanksgiving Day she arrived at her brother's house not knowing how she was going to help with the dinner, as she usually did. All she could do was sink down onto the carpet and play with her adorable niece and nephew. After dinner, Sunny planted herself at the sink and managed to do the dishes without even moving her foot.

The next day Sunny went back to her brother's house, prepared to apologize for being so unhelpful with dinner. She feared that she had alienated Dana, her sister-in-law, by not doing her share of the work, so she was surprised when Dana met her at the door and threw her arms around her, thanking her for not coming into the kitchen while she was cooking. "All I wanted is my kitchen to myself while someone else plays with the children, and you did that for me. That is the best thing that could happen to me when I have to make a big dinner." Sunny smiled to herself, hugged Dana back, and learned that she should have asked, during all these years of helping, whether she was in fact in the way.

How Can Two Sisters Support Their Aging Aunt?

Gloria and Lily, two sisters, never had a conversation about who would take care of their aging aunt. Gloria had taken care of her father while he was dying, and felt that Lily had not done her share. Now Auntie was dying. Lily lived quite close to their aunt, so Gloria was taken aback to learn that her sister was doing nothing to help care for their aunt. Gloria scowled, decided to skip her book club meeting, drove across town, and checked in on her aunt. Gloria could see that the refrigerator needed cleaning and stocking, and the laundry had not been done. Week after week Gloria helped her aunt and did not talk to Lily about her anger. Gloria finally realized that, once again, she was the responsible sister, but this time she decided to say something to Lily.

Gloria waited until her anger was not raging. She wanted to stay calm and engage Lily in the caretaking, not alienate her. Gloria used her meditation practice to help her return to her center, calm her anger, and find her way to working well with Lily. After planning what she was going to say, Gloria called Lily. "I want to stay friends over this," she said. "I don't want to make trouble between us, but

I have something on my mind about Auntie. I am going over there once a week, and I think she needs more attention. You live quite close to her. I need your help with her. Can you give her some time? Or should we hire someone to care for her?"

Lily was shaken. She did not like being a caretaker. She had been relieved that Gloria was again shouldering the burden. She thought Gloria liked tending to older people. Lily said: "I am sorry to have put this all on you. I thought you liked caring for Auntie. I have not done my share. I think we need to figure out a way to care for her so we enjoy our time with her and with each other. Maybe we should meet there once a week and together do what needs to be done."

Gloria was not satisfied with this suggestion. She thought Lily was only thinking of herself. Gloria would still be going weekly. She felt unappreciated and her anger rose. This was just like Lily, wanting to arrange things her way without understanding that not enough of a concession had been made. Gloria said she would try Lily's plan for a few weeks, but then asked Lily if she would visit Auntie this week, as Gloria needed a break. Gloria spoke in a neutral, undemanding way, and Lily said yes.

If Gloria had chosen to have this conversation with Lily when she first learned that their aunt needed help, she would have avoided her resentment. Instead of making assumptions, Lily also might have asked Gloria how she felt about having cared for their father and now caring for their aunt. Assumptions often lead to misunderstandings. They tend to include the hopes and wishes of one person, which often are the opposite of what is in the mind of the other person. But a conversation can lead two people to the true feelings and desires of each other. Surprising information and solutions can arise when we get passed our assumptions.

How Do I Handle My Brother's Misuse of Drugs and Money?

"I am not coming for brunch if Sidney is going to be there," my friend Anna said to her mother. This was a new position for Anna, who was always the pleasant one, never making demands, always trying to keep peace in the family. Now, after more than twenty years of being the "good one," she was beginning to set limits to protect herself.

Anna is the older of two children; Sidney is three and half years younger. As children of two successful professionals, they spent a lot of time together when they were younger, playing, inventing games, watching TV, and enjoying each other's company. When Anna went off to college, and Sidney started high school, he began to change. He was smoking a lot of marijuana, as he had throughout junior high school, but he was also bragging to Anna on the phone about trying stronger drugs. She was not amused but did not say anything to him. He seemed to be getting decent grades. As the years went by and Sidney's drug use continued, Anna graduated from college, moved to another city, started to publish a magazine, and fell in love. She went home a few times a year for holidays, and Sidney was always there, but Anna did not have time to focus on him. When they were together, the family talked about news, politics, and work, but seldom about themselves.

Sidney graduated from college and went to work in a high-powered advertising agency. Always good looking and charming, he moved up in his profession, changing agencies from time to time. But the time came when his job changes were numerous and always horizontal. Sidney explained that his frequent job changes were never because he had done something wrong. Anna began to realize that cocaine was playing a big part in his life. Eventually Sidney began asking Anna for money to tide him over between jobs. She helped him out the first few times, but soon she began to understand the severity of her brother's addiction. She grew to dislike spending time with him. When she told her parents what she had surmised about Sidney, they denied he had a drug problem. When she refused to loan Sidney money, he was rude and angry. Anna became furious with her parents for denying the problem and continuing to support her brother's drug use with money. She was tired of her mother asking her to be a go-between. She did not want to come away from every family event feeling abused and powerless.

At last Anna spoke to her parents and set some parameters: "I love Sidney. I love you. My anger is getting in the way of my relationship with him. I can't be around him as he is. I am too upset by what he is doing to you and to me and to his family. I will not talk with you any more about Sidney. I will not come to your house when Sidney is there. I will not invite Sidney to my home until he addresses his drug and money issues." Anna let the family know that she would be pleased to reestablish a relationship with Sidney after he entered rehab and was clean and sober for six months. She would not see him under any other conditions.

Sometimes you have to be firm and strong in order to come back to an intimate connection with a loved one. This may feel harsh, and certainly takes courage. Anna knew that to protect herself and not be an accomplice in Sidney's addiction, she needed some space. She also realized that she needed to protect herself from the pain of encounters with Sidney and conversations with her parents about Sidney. She did not want the separation to be permanent. She stated clearly the conditions under which she would be willing to be with Sidney again, and she hoped her parents would learn from her example how to set their own limits. Anna set boundaries to protect herself, then calmly described the conditions of her self-protection to her parents and to Sidney. Because of this, she was able to sustain a relationship with her parents and remain hopeful that so Sidney would receive help for his addiction.

Should I Confront My Sister about Her Drinking?

Anita's older sister Jane was drinking again. She was drinking a lot. Anita lived far away from her, so she could easily ignore the facts. But when Jane came to stay with Anita and attend the wedding of Anita's only daughter, Anita saw Jane sipping wine in the kitchen early in the morning, and throughout the day the level of wine in the bottle went down and down. Anita was normally the plain-talking sister, while Jane wanted to keep the peace at all costs. Because of the wedding Anita had her mind on many other things; she did not have the energy to confront her sister. Instead, she spoke to her Jane's oldest son Ted, and asked him what he thought. Ted agreed that his mother had a problem and said he would find out about rehabilitation programs that might be appropriate for her. Ted followed through on his word to Anita and found a residential detoxification program about fifty miles from their home.

Anita traveled to Jane's house to help Ted and Ken, Jane's husband, inform Jane about their concerns and their hopes. The three of them went to Jane and told her she was drinking too much and they were worried about her. First they spoke of their love. Then they spoke at length of their worries and their desires. They wanted Jane to live a long and healthy life with them. Finally they told her what they had been planning for her. They knew she would be furious, they said, but they had to do this for themselves; otherwise they would feel irresponsible and uncaring.

Jane left the room a few times. She became very angry at one point, but Ted, Anita, and Ken sat quietly and patiently. They said they could see why she would be angry, and they were not leaving until she had heard them. They were here because they cared, they reminded her. After a while, Jane became quieter and rather sullen.

Anita told Jane that Ted had arranged for her to enter a program to get the alcohol out of her system. Anita said she would take her there the next morning. Jane said it was too soon. Jane sat, twisting her hands, and then—much to their surprise—she went upstairs and packed her bag. She cancelled her engagements for the next month and got into the car. She was rather proud to be going.

The family thanked Jane as well. They told her how proud they were of her, how courageous she was, how much they realized she had done for them, and that they were so glad to see her looking so well. Jane felt appreciated for the first time in many years. She had a struggle ahead of her to remain sober, but this time she felt supported in her effort, not alone in her life.

Family interventions designed to move a loved one toward caring for herself seldom work this well. Resistance, anger, feelings of betrayal, the power of denial—all get in the way of a decision in favor of health. Repeated conversations are usually necessary. The power of the love from her family rather than confrontational directives convinced Jane to enter a detoxification program.

How Can We Fairly Divide the Estate?

Colin and Walt grew up in Wisconsin. Their parents also owned vacation property on the shores of Lake Michigan, where all the cousins learned to swim and as teenagers had summer romances. When their mother died, she left Colin and Walt the property: two beautiful lakefront houses, two docks, and a boathouse. The brothers had very different ideas of how to manage the inherited property. One house was very large and sumptuous; the other was small and simple. Walt, the older brother, wanted to sell the property. Colin wanted to fix it up and rent it out, retaining the right to use it in July each year.

After several heated arguments, the brothers "divorced" each other. They no longer spent holidays together; their children, who were spread across the country, no longer summered together on the lakefront property. Colin and his family retained use of the small cottage. He rented the large house without redecorating it, and he split the rent with Walt. The large family reunions on the lake ended. After he clearly stated he had no interest in the property, Walt did not communicate with Colin. Each brother was in great pain. Colin wanted to reconcile; Walt did not. Both parties needed to be willing to negotiate to accommodate their different wishes or reconciliation would not happen. Neither brother was taking into account the pain their estrangement caused for the rest of the family.

Three years after their mother's death, the deadlock continued. In three separate letters to his brother, Colin expressed his desire to talk; he offered to meet with a therapist or mediator of his brother's choosing. Three times Colin wrote that the relationship with Walt meant more to him than the property. He wanted their children to grow up together, as all the cousins had in his generation. Three times Colin received no answer. He wrote a fourth time. Again Colin stressed the value of the relationship. He wrote about his love for the property, about he desire to model a loving sibling relationship for his children. He asked his brother if receiving half the rent was satisfactory and, if not, how he would prefer to handle the situation. He reported that repairs had to be made and they should be splitting the costs. He offered to drop the redecorating idea if Walt would agree to keep the property in good repair, rent it out, and ultimately will it to all their children.

Walt was not happy with this arrangement. He wanted to retire and needed the money that would come with the sale of the property. He knew Colin did not have the money to buy him out. Walt decided to seek the advice of a lawyer regarding his rights, his obligations, and possible solutions. In hearing himself describe the situation, Walt realized that he would have to work directly with Colin on solutions. He did not miss Colin; he did not yearn to reconnect with him. He just wanted to make this a business decision that would give them both some relief from the stalemate. He did not care about the relationships among the next generation of cousins. Walt decided to call Colin. "We need to find a way to get out of this impasse," he told his brother. "I would still like to sell the property and take my share of the money. I know you can't buy me out and that you want the property."

In the end, the brothers worked out an economic solution in which Colin was able to buy out his brother by mortgaging both his city house and the lakefront property. Colin had enough money left to fix up both houses and the docks. He was able to rent the big house for enough money to pay back the mortgages over time. Colin and Walt did not reconcile, but they established a quiet divorce, not an angry one. There is still the possibility that they will reconnect later.

Should I Invite My Brother to Live with Me during His Divorce?

When he was fifty-eight, with their youngest child out of college, Rick and his wife Madeline split up. They had been married thirty years. Rick had just begun to look forward to a more leisurely life with Madeline. When Madeline realized she could support herself as a potter, she asked Rick for a divorce. He was shocked. Unprepared, he did not know where to turn.

Rick had to face starting over—finding a place to live, making new friends, dating—just when he felt very lost and ashamed that his marriage had failed. He had not even noticed that his relationship with his wife was disintegrating. He knew their lives had gone in different directions. Their connection to each other was no longer a cause for celebration. They were both worn down by their differentness and their idiosyncrasies. Neither was going to change, and neither was tolerant or amused by the other's ways. He did not press Madeline to go into counseling.

Rick felt quite lost. He needed someone to talk to so he called his brother Jerome. He and Jerome had not been close for years, but he knew Jerome would listen. And Jerome knew Madeline. In fact, Rick was sure that Jerome and his wife Julie had never liked Madeline, that she was a factor in the distance between the brothers. Besides asking Jerome to help him mull over his situation, he also asked to come and live with Jerome and Julie. He told Jerome this would be temporary, just until he could figure out how much money he had, where to live, and what he was going to do with his life. Although Jerome was in a particularly busy, productive period in his life, he said, "Yes, you can come and live with us for a time." He did not worry that Rick would outstay his welcome, but he *did* fear that having another person in his house for several months would negatively affect his relationship with Julia. The three of them would need to talk about responsibilities and possible areas of conflict. They would need an open conversation to set the parameters for sharing a kitchen, a house, and perhaps a social life.

Jerome began the conversation with Rick like this: "We need to talk. All three of us. I want to know what your expectations are for the time you are here. I want to think out loud with you about how we do this so we are all comfortable. I want to be able to return to this conversation and revise some of our conclusions, as needed. I want our time together to go well. I hope this will be a time we get reacquainted. I hope this time with us will allow you to go ahead with your life. I want to be responsive to you but not overwhelmed by your needs."

Rick responded in a similarly calm and thoughtful way: "I too want this to go well. I don't want to be in the way or be a burden to you. I would like to work out a way to be helpful around the house, pay you some rent, and hang out with you, but not all the time. I hope you will tell me clearly when I am welcome to join you and Julia and when you need time to yourselves. I hope we can talk about the arrangements whenever we need to. I don't want tensions to build up. I have a tendency to put off difficult conversations. I know this from my thirty-plus years with Madeline. This time I want to keep up with what is bothering me and tell you nicely. I am so appreciative that you are willing to have me stay with you. I found it hard to ask. Thanks for responding so quickly and positively. I would like to move in next month. How is that for you?"

For two months, Rick, Jerome, and Julia lived together. Every morning, each one went out to work. They helped themselves to breakfast and cleaned up their own dishes. Many nights Rick joined Jerome and Julia for dinner. They enjoyed each other's company. When Jerome and Julia wanted time on their own, they went upstairs to their bedroom. As the divorce proceedings moved toward resolution, Rick began to look for a condo. The house he owned with Madeline was on the market, and he would soon have money for a down payment.

After Rick moved out of Jerome and Julia's house, he continued to visit them often. Jerome spent some evenings at Rick's condo, listening to him talk about making new friends and how different the dating scene is after thirty years of marriage. Eventually Rick joined a singles group. His brother's support helped him through a difficult time in his life. Their conversations made the interlude work smoothly for both men and brought them closer.

Do I Have to Welcome My Sister-in-Law into My Marriage?

Zak and Amy, brother and sister, spent a lot of time together while growing up and as single adults. After Zak married Sarah, his affection for his sister aroused some jealous feelings in his new wife. Sarah wanted to be as intimate with her husband as he seemed to be with Amy, and she did not like him spending a lot of time with her new sister-in-law. But Zak felt his sister needed him because she was still single, and he often wanted to include her in their weekend plans despite his wife's quiet complaints. Zak often felt he had to choose: his wife or his sister. Either way, one of the two women would feel hurt and left out.

Zak finally decided he needed to speak about his feelings of being torn in two—with his wife and his sister together so they would both feel included. He needed to talk about his love for both of them, his understanding of the problem, and his desire to please them both. He also needed to speak about his own needs. Here is what he told them: "I adore both of you. I would like to have you both live with me, but I know that would not work for Sarah. And probably you, dear sister, don't want that either. I want you both to feel you have time with me, and I want you to get to know each other. I think you would like each other. I want more time with Sarah, and I want you, Amy, to have more time with Sarah, too. I would like to have some time for myself. At the moment, I feel like I have to be with one or both of you whenever I have a free moment."

The two women looked at each other. They had both been so busy wanting Zak, they had not considered getting to know each other. They realized that because of their competition for Zak's time, they had distrusted each other. Perhaps they had things in common. Zak was wise to remove himself from the middle of the tug-of-war between his wife and his sister. As the women's friendship grew, they began to spend more time together, sometimes even without Zak. Soon Zak could spend time with his wife without feeling guilty about his sister. And Sarah and Zak found that including Amy in their life was no longer an effort. Feeling appreciated, Amy in turn gave the newlyweds more time alone and soon became the loving auntie to Zak and Sarah's baby.

Not only a sibling, but also a parent, a child from a former marriage, or a close friend can become part of a family dynamic that pulls one partner away from the other. Addressing the imbalance directly becomes necessary as a way of maintaining loving family relationships.

Conclusion

Siblings are an often overlooked, but important relationship. The death of a sibling can be as devastating as the death of a spouse. Though some people lose contact with siblings, the memories they share still play an important part in their lives. For siblings who stay in contact, the issues that arise are more intense than with friends, and walking away from conflict is more difficult. The family history shared by siblings may include painful memories, with the reflective interpretations of these memories being very different. One may have been the victim of the other. Often the desire to be different from a sibling intensifies judgments and interactions. Many of the choices we make in life are because a sibling did or did not do that same thing. The subtle influence of siblings is part of who we become and how we present ourselves in the world. Conversations with siblings take the same care and consideration as those in any other close relationship. The childish bickering and blurting out of any and all feelings cannot continue into adulthood if a loving connection is desired.

CHAPTER 12

Using Intergenerational Conversations to Make Decisions at the End of Life

As the end of life approaches, family members have one last opportunity to connect in a deeper way. This is a time of change, uncertainty, and, hopefully, love and tenderness. Children now have a chance to say thank you to a dying parent and to give in a way that only occurs at the end of life. The more consciousness we bring to this time, the better chance we have for intimate moments and for learning the wisdom the older person has accumulated through a lifetime of experiences. And when we help our elders move into death with grace, we are also giving them a chance to offer one last lesson to the next generation. Not all deaths offer this opportunity. Pain may overtake grace and unconsciousness may block words, but when a loved one is slowly dying, we can reach out with goodbyes and expressions of appreciation.

As grandparents and parents grow older, and their capacity to care for themselves decreases, many adult children choose to become the caregiver, the support person, and the decision maker. Others may pull away, ignore the change in their parents, or hire others to do the work. The major end-of-life decisions about housing, care, wills, and medical interventions all need to be made primarily by the aging person, often in conjunction with her children. When an older person is no longer able to manage his affairs, the children must step in. Diplomacy, tact, and patience are called for at this point. The loss of physical ability, independence, and clarity of thought may increase the irritability of the person who is aging. To avoid regrets later for things said in haste or for actions not taken, attention, patience, and compassion need to be brought to each encounter.

Will I Make a Timely Decision to Stop Driving?

Before telling me his experience, David admitted that pride came before his decision to stop driving. Every five years, to renew his driver's license David was required to take a written test. At age eighty-nine he passed with flying colors. The last of his group to be driving, he chauffeured his friends wherever they needed to go. For the next five years he thought he had the driving situation well in hand. The pride came when he again passed the test at age ninety-four. But a year later David began having mini-strokes. The first was in a restaurant, surrounded by his friends. He passed out, and later he realized some minutes had passed that he could not account for. He drove for a few more days and then had another episode—luckily, inside his home. After his second stroke, David decided he had to stop driving. "I can't jeopardize myself, my wife, and the other drivers," he told me.

"This is the worst thing that could happen to me," David told his son on the phone. Then he changed his mind and said, "No, the worst is what is happening now, with your mother's shoulder hurting. She can't drive either. I guess the time has come to move to Oak Grove. We can leave our home and move to the next stage. I have made changes before and I am grateful for every morning I wake up."

David Jr. was very relieved that his father clearly recognized his next life stage. He would not need to intervene. He hoped that when he was his father's age, he too would be able to make changes as gracefully as his father.

How Can I Convince My Elderly Parents to Stop Driving?

When Nan, age eighty-eight, drove thirty miles past her usual exit and ended up in Iowa instead of Illinois, her three sons began to talk about the hazards of their lost mother driving around the countryside. They were not yet ready to reverse the roles and tell their mother what she could and could not do. They felt bewildered and they knew they had to attend to this. They talked for two weeks. Finally, the wife of Nan's oldest son called her mother-in-law, of whom she was very fond, and said to her, "I know this must be on your mind, and I know what a hard decision it is, but all of your children hope you will stop driving."

Remembering the lost feeling she recently had while driving, Nan simply said, "You're right. Okay." She liked the matter-of-fact, straightforward way that her loving daughter-in-law had made the recommendation that she stop driving. She did not feel deprived of her autonomy.

This process does not usually go so easily. I have often been told that giving up driving is much more difficult for men than for women. I asked my cousin Jonathon how he had handled this issue with his mother and father, my Aunt Margaret and Uncle Barry, especially knowing how Barry was very attached to his automobiles. Jonathon told me that he had recently visited his parents in Arizona, where they were wintering. Because of his job and other family obligations, he hadn't seen his parents in a year.

His parents had rented the same condo for the previous nine winters. Jonathon and his family were staying at a nearby Holiday Inn. The first evening of the visit they all met for dinner at the hotel. After their meal Jonathon decided to go back to the condo with his parents, while his wife Donna stayed with their children at the hotel. He wanted some quiet time with his father and mother without all the distractions that his family created. Driving from the hotel to the condo was an easy quarter of a mile on a road his parents had been driving for nine years. They used the road to drive everywhere—golf, shopping, restaurants—but this night Barry overshot the condo driveway and then, swearing about the poor signage, backed up onto the busy road without looking and correctly entered the condo's parking area.

Jonathon had been aware during dinner that his father was not participating in the conversation as much as usual and had to ask a couple of times to be filled in on what one of his grandchildren had said. Jonathon started to wonder: Was his father's hearing failing? Or his mind? His mother had not said anything during the weekly calls, but then Dad was always listening on the extension in the den, even when he did not say much. Jonathon realized for the first time that his parents were less capable than he, and that he might be called upon to help them in new ways. This felt uncomfortable because he still turned to his father for advice, especially about cars. What was he supposed to say or do as an only child now that his parents were less able to cope with their lives?

Once they were settled on the couches in the living room of their condo, Jonathon tentatively and cautiously brought up the difficult subject of driving. Knowing that his father's ego, sense of power, and identity rested on the steering wheel of his car, Jonathon was aware that he had to be careful. He also remembered his father's temper, especially the outbursts when he was a child. "Night driving seems to be getting harder for you, Dad," Jonathon said to his father. "Maybe you need to let Mom drive at night down here where you are less familiar with the roads. I noticed you overshot the driveway tonight."

Barry turned red and shouted at Jonathon, "Don't you ever talk to me like that." That roar had silenced Jonathon over and over as a child. At that moment, he wanted to give up, but he knew that to feel good about himself and his responsibility to his parents, he needed to stick with the conversation as calmly as possible. What was more important, he asked himself, his relationship with his father or the safety of both his parents?

Barry got up and stomped off into the bedroom. Jonathon wished his mother would give him some support, but she said, "Now see, you've upset your father." While Barry was undressing for bed, he continued to yell.

Jonathon stood in the doorway of the bedroom, growing angry himself. "I hope you will consider what I said," he finally roared back to his father, and then banged out of the condo. "I sounded just like him," Jonathan told me. "Am I really as loud as he is? Do I roar at my children? What am I to do?"

The next day Barry told Jonathon that he lay awake all night. He was frightened. What if his vision was failing? What if he did have to give up night driving? He knew he couldn't see the road signs at night, that the long piercing rays of approaching car lights were blurred and making him squint with discomfort. He knew he could not let Margaret touch his car—that was for sure. She was starting to have little accidents with her own car, which so far they had not considered to be a serious issue.

Jonathon had a sleepless night too. He had not been prepared for the changes in his father nor for the conversation. He did not know whether he should pursue the subject in the morning or leave it alone with the hope that had planted a seed. Should he apologize for yelling? He had not meant to do that, and he felt bad about it. Should he talk to his mother alone?

The next morning Barry reminded Jonathon that he was at his best behind the wheel of his car. He needed to drive to Arizona in the winter. He still wanted to play golf. If he didn't drive, how would he get to the golf course? How would he get out to have his monthly cigar? He proudly said to me, "Here I am, eighty-six, nothing hurts. I can walk eighteen holes of golf and swing as well at the beginning of the game as at the end. I am playing as well as ever. The doctor says my ticker is that of a man of seventy-five. So I lose my wallet and keys and glasses; everyone does that."

In the morning, as Margaret and Barry watched their grandchildren play in the hotel swimming pool, Jonathon did manage to say, "I am sorry I raised my voice last night. I hope you are thinking about what I said."

"Yes," said Barry, and looked away.

When Jonathon returned home, he managed to turn his attention to this difficult task. He went to the bookstore and the library to find books on aging. He began to admit to himself that one day he would age, and he did not want his children to be as stuck as he now felt. He talked to friends. He called a social worker in Scranton, where his parents lived, and asked about her services and about any outside resources that could be tapped as his parents' needs increased. What did she charge? How did she approach her elderly clients, all of whom, presumably, wanted to maintain as much independence as possible?

Jonathon also called his father's doctor, who told him that half his practice consisted of people over eighty, and he was often receiving calls like this from others concerned for their parents. He told Jonathon that he used to approach the topic of driving with his patients by asking, "Do you think you need to stop driving?" When he realized that no one ever said yes, he knew he needed another approach. He next tried telling them that a concerned family member had called, but that created anger and blame in the family. Now, he told Jonathon, he sits down with each patient and asks a series of carefully worded, very specific questions:

- Do you feel your reflexes are slower than ten years ago?
- Do you have insurance?

- Have you had any car accidents? If so, how many?
- When was your last written driving test?
- When was your last behind-the-wheel driving test?
- When were your eyes last tested?
- Do you drive at night? How is that?
- Do you see pedestrians or do they surprise you?
- How often do you miss your exit off of the freeway?
- Can you read all the signs in time to appropriately react?
- Have you ever been lost in a familiar part of town?
- How far are you driving at a time?
- Do you ever secretly worry about your driving?
- What will you do when you can't drive anymore?

This doctor found that when his patients begin to hear their own replies to these questions, they also begin to ask what they might do to deal with this change in their lifestyle. After his patients have time to reflect, the doctor tells them what he knows from helping other patients in the same situation:

- Some people hire a driver a few days a week.
- Some open a charge account with a local taxi.
- Some have younger friends and neighbors who take them out.
- Some get live-in help who can drive them where they wish to go.
- Some decide to move into a retirement community when they choose to quit driving.
- Some move into a small apartment on a bus route.
- I am here to talk to you about this whenever you want to.
- I would hate to see you wait until you have an accident to make a change.

The next Sunday Jonathon called his parents, as he usually did, and opened the conversation in a very unusual manner:

- How are you doing with your aging process?
- How are you feeling about the changes in your mind and body?
- I need your help for when I get older. What can you tell me about it all?

Barry ranted a bit about how awful getting old was becoming—friends dying, facing his own mortality, losing his independence, never knowing when or how the end would come, worrying about Margaret, who did not know how to pay the bills.

Jonathan listened. He listened, knowing he would one day say the same things, unless he found a better way to ease into the inevitable. Toward the end of the conversation Jonathon thanked his father for his reflections, as he too would die and he wanted to handle that stage of his life with grace.

Jonathon was pleased with himself for not pushing for more immediate results, for opening the conversation and then just listening. He would continue this subject in a few weeks. His hope was that his father would just take charge of the situation and give Jonathon the role of supporting his decisions.

The questions Barry's doctor asked his patients, along with those Barry asked his father, can be asked by any friend, spouse, or child in the same situation. You don't need to ask all the questions; a few may be enough. Like Jonathon, you may not be ready to categorically state that your parents or grandparents can't drive anymore, preferring to help them become aware of their increasing limitations so they can make a reasoned choice for themselves in a timely fashion.

When Should I Visit My Aging Mother Who Lives in Another State?

Vince has been in a complicated dance with his mother April. Vince was the first of all his siblings to leave home, and he also moved the farthest away. He never seemed to have the time to visit his mother, so every year or so April flew to California to visit him. She rarely saw her grandchildren and shared in their lives only from a distance. She wrote letters to Vince, who was not an only child. April also had three daughters, and Adele, the youngest girl, always saw Vince as their mother's favorite. She often talked about him in conversation with her sisters, who lived nearby, as though to keep him with them in his absence.

Now in his sixties and retired, Vince has written to his mother, telling her he wants to come for a visit. April, now ninety-five, cannot travel to see him, yet she has told him not to come. Adele and her sisters were stunned when their mother told them, after all these years of worship, that she didn't want Vince to come. "Why not let Vince come?" they asked April. They offered to do all the work—make a big dinner, plan a reunion with all the relatives, including not only April's grandchildren but also her great-grandchildren, Vince's boyhood friends, even the neighbors who had known him when he was a kid. But April continued to say no with these blunt words: "This feels too much like I am dying and Vince is coming to say goodbye."

Vince wanted to visit his mother to resolve his own issues. He thought about just showing up, but realized that seemed too self-serving. He decided that instead of asking he would just tell her he was coming. Because of his clarity, she saw she had no choice in the matter and was able to accept his visit.

When Vince was finally with his mother, he spoke directly to her fear:

- I think you did not want me to come because my visit means you are dying.
- I would like to come several more times before you do die, not because you are dying but because I want to spend some time with you.

- How often would you like me to come?
- How can I make my visits a pleasure for you and not a burden?
- Talking about death is difficult but it is something we can try to discuss.

Vince dared to enter into one of the most difficult conversations of all, one that recognizes mortality. He tried to speak with love and openness, not fear and denial. His mother was touched that Vince was coming to visit despite her protestations. She had secretly wanted to see him but was afraid to ask him to come. She was able to say to him, "Thank you." And as April approached the end of her life, she was able to call Vince and ask him to be with her during her last days, which he really wanted to do.

How Can I Convince My Parents to Accept Outside Help?

Ada's father Eric had a heart attack. Three weeks later, Ada arrived home to find her father bedridden and her mother Cheryl taking care of everything. At eighty-five, Cheryl looked as worn out as Eric, though she was not complaining about the care giving. She had thrown herself into it.

Ada was a child who never criticized her parents, but she knew the time had come to intervene in their lives. Her father would soon be up and walking but his doctor had recommended that he no longer be driving. Ada also found that her father was very forgetful. Even her mother was more forgetful than Ada remembered. She did not know whether that was from anxiety about her new responsibilities as a caregiver or senility coming on.

Ada helped as much as she could, but Cheryl would not let her do much. Ada called Services for the Elderly to find out what equipment for the bathroom and the bedroom would help her father maintain his independence and remain safe. Ada was able to help her father in and out of the shower. She took over driving to get groceries, leaving her mother to take care of her father. Within a week Ada knew she could not return to her husband Gary and their children without finding additional help for her parents. In the past Cheryl would have very abruptly rejected any advice and Ada felt this had not changed. What should she say?

Ada spent an hour telling a childhood friend about her dilemma. Together they came up with and practiced the words. Ada said, "Mother, I don't know how you do this, taking care of Daddy all day, all by yourself, seven days a week. I don't think I could do it for Gary. I would need some time to rest, to remember who I am, to recharge my energy in some way—even if it's just with a manicure—so I could go back and be with him again. To have to stop my life so completely for someone else would be very hard for me." Then Ada paused and waited. Cheryl said nothing and wandered off. Ada stayed, reading on the couch where she had been.

The next day Cheryl approached Ada: "I think you *would* take care of Gary this way. I did not know I could be the caregiver I have become, and yet here I am. You just do what you have to, that's all. This is what needs doing right now. I don't think I could leave him with strangers."

Ada slowly raised an eyebrow. Her mother frowned. Ada did not want to press her mother. She knew Cheryl would continue thinking about what had been said. Ada wanted her mother to make the decision and to feel she had made the decision herself.

Cheryl picked up the conversation just before Ada had to leave: "Well, I guess a person is not a stranger after the first time she comes. I think if I had someone two afternoons a week for a while, I might be more pleasant to your father when I am with him. I am rather short with him sometimes. Where do I find someone?"

Ada found the local Visiting Nurse Agency and some private home-nursing companies in the yellow pages. She began to research the cost, the various services offered, the method of selection of the workers, and the insurance situation. She learned that her father's insurance would partially pay for in-home help. Ada helped her mother interview agency representatives and nurses. By the time Ada left for home, they had chosen a nurse, who had come twice to the house. Cheryl had gone out once, and Eric had slept the whole time she was away.

Patience and loving conversations brought Erica and Don to a similarly happy ending. At ninety-three, Erica insisted on living alone, but going up and down the stairs of her three-story house was beginning to be difficult. Until two years earlier Erica's role in the neighborhood had been to drive older people to appointments; now she was dependent on others for rides.

Erica's son Don came from Long Island for monthly visits with his mother in New Jersey. He had already noticed the lack of cleaning, but now the dust and the newspapers and the trash were really piling up. A few weeks later Don returned with his daughter, and together the three of them talked about what kind of help Erica would need during the coming years. "We want you to have help with the shopping and cooking," Don said to his mother. "We want someone in the house to help you on the days you are tired. You have done an amazing job taking care of yourself all these years. We want you to be able to take it easy now that you are ninety-three. *For our sakes,* we want you to get help at least part time, to clean and do some cooking."

At first Erica said she did not want anyone in the house and even if she did, she did not know how to go about finding someone. Finally she admitted that she was embarrassed for another woman to see how she was living. She loved her son and her granddaughter, and she knew they were right, but she did not say so.

A few visits later Don reminded his mother of the conversation. "Mother," he said, "I am still concerned about you living here on your own. I am going to look for someone." This was an important step because Erica was no longer able to do this job herself. On his way home Don stopped in a nearby senior residence, where he talked to the receptionist and met with a few of the aides. He asked if anybody wanted ten hours of extra work each week. One of the aides was delighted by the opportunity. Don arranged for her to work two hours each day, tidying up, buying food, doing light cooking. Now, he thought, my mother can slow down and read her books and her newspapers.

Erica's ability to see the reality of the situation and Don's framing the issue as his problem, not his mother's, made her able to listen. "I am concerned," he said, not, "You have to get help." His gentle insistence and ingenuity in arranging for help made this conversation useful for both of them.

How Can I Care for My Wife When She Is a Reluctant Patient?

Relationships change a lot during an extended partnership. The caregiver and the receiver of care tend to shift roles from time to time, but sometimes the needs of one person clearly outweigh the needs of the other. How to ask and receive, how to give, and how to keep on going can become difficult to determine. The answers can lead to an increased distance from loved ones or—with awareness, kindness, and compassion—the most challenging moments can lead to closeness and even more love between partners.

When Marilyn needed to be in the hospital for three weeks of chemotherapy after many years of living with leukemia, she and her husband Fred did not know that their ability to respond to each other's needs would be part of the challenge. The most difficult night, she told me, was early in her hospital stay when she and Fred both cried and cried, saying how they wanted to please each other but could not do it. Marilyn did not want Fred to have to sit with her all day, every day. She had arranged for different friends to visit every day for a few hours. Fred could work on his book or in his garden, or he could relax in the morning when she wanted to be alone to read and sleep and get cleaned up. She had invited her friends to visit in the early afternoon and then asked Fred to be with her through dinner and the evening hours, when she knew she would be most lonely. This made sense to her and seemed not too demanding of him, but Fred took her suggestion as rejection. He felt Marilyn was pushing him away. Marilyn felt he was not listening to her need for alone time. Fred felt useless. He felt he could be helpful by coming in and out during the day. For Marilyn, too much was going on.

Only a week into her hospital stay did Marilyn and Fred began to talk about this. They were not pleasant, controlled, or well-mannered.

Marilyn insisted her needs should come first, and Fred should do it her way.

Fred said he wanted to do everything for her, and that she was cutting him out.

Marilyn groaned. She again told him that she needed time to be alone.

They cried some more.

Fred told Marilyn he needed to hear that she wanted him there.

Marilyn quietly told Fred that she did need him to be there, that she wanted him there, but that she also needed time with no one there.

Fred said he needed to see her first thing each morning because he worried all night.

Marilyn then understood what was driving him.

He better understood her needs, too.

Fred came less often. Marilyn was glad to see him in the morning.

One night toward the end of her hospital stay, Fred slept in Marilyn's room on a narrow Naugahyde pullout chair with sheets and blankets that kept slipping onto the floor. Marilyn loved having him there.

Having a conscious conversation does *not* mean having no hot feelings, not yelling, not crying, not speaking the whole truth. It means doing all these things in a spirit of openness, with a desire to heal, and without self-righteousness or blaming.

How Can I Help My Mother Move to a Senior Residence?

Paula lived alone. Both of her children lived out of town and her husband was deceased. Paula's eyesight was failing and she recognized that to stay in her home she needed more services than she could afford. Even the smallest tasks were difficult: finding her scissors, writing a legible note, reading her utility bill. She was always tilting her head this way and that, trying to use what light she could see to find her way. She was no longer able to read after dark; she even found watching TV very taxing. She tried listening to recorded books, but it was not the same as reading. Although her situation was becoming untenable, she did not want to let go of her current lifestyle. Making a change seemed too monumental. She did have a few friends scattered through a few of the town's senior residences. How bad would it be to live in one? How would she ever be able to decide which?

One day Paula called her daughter Darlene and started the conversation by asking if this might be a good time to talk. Darlene agreed the timing was good, and then Paula admitted her vision problem was making life difficult, but she also felt reluctant to move. For the first time she admitted that she was leaving the stove on, losing things, and feeling disoriented from time to time. One of her fears, Paula said, was that if she was having this much trouble at home, a new place where she really did not know her way around might be worse.

Darlene listened. She even found herself feeling sorry for her mother. She tried to imagine how she will feel when she reaches her mother's stage in life. She said to her mother, "This sounds so hard. May I help you with this decision?" Darlene did not back away or wish her mother had not called. She found herself moved by her mother's dilemma and wanting to help. Paula felt Darlene's concern for her. They began to work together.

Darlene located a social worker where Paula lived who specialized in working with aging people. She knew the local resources and she had experience helping older people make major transitions. The social worker took Paula to look at senior residences with special support for vision-impaired seniors. Most importantly, at each facility Paula was able to talk with some of the residents. Learning about all the social activities made her realize she not have to depend on television to pass the time.

The social worker had handled such cases many times and knew how to help Paula make a choice, move, settle in, and adjust to the change. She was able to engage the part of Paula that knew she had to move. She appealed to Paula's rational self, while comforting the part of her that wished this move were not happening. "I am sure it is very hard to make this move, to leave a place you love," the social worker told Paula. "Yet we both know this change has become necessary."

Paula relaxed. She thanked Darlene for connecting her to the social worker. Darlene and she had an amicable, warm, friendly, and mutually supportive relationship that continued to grow through the remainder of Paula's life. In this case, Paula was the first to open the conversation about assisted living, and a social worker was the key to a smooth transition. In another case, only after two winters of hearing her mother talk about her loneliness was Libby able to help her mother make the decision to move to a senior residence. Libby began the transition by arranging to take her mother Milly on official tours of several senior residences. They looked at the places where Milly had already visited friends, a place with a culturally and racially mixed population, and a place that was faith-based. Some offered only meal service and light cleaning, others offered a continuum of care until the grave. Milly would be able to keep her own furniture in some places; in others she would be able to use their furniture.

After visiting each facility, Libby asked her mother: "What do you like about this place? What don't you like? Did you like our tour guide? Do you have any friends who live here? What do you think of the social programs, the dining room, and the living spaces? Can you imagine living here?"

Milly was able to distinguish between what she liked and didn't like about the various programs and places. A few days later Libby placed Milly's name on the waiting list for the place that was clearly her favorite, a fairly new facility that she had seen being built, and where two people she knew lived.

Milly was expecting a few months to go by before an apartment became available for her, which was fine. She was not quite ready to move. However, just a week later Milly was involved in an automobile accident. The residence also reported that an apartment was available. Milly could move immediately. Libby felt relieved. She had been doing a lot of housekeeping and personal care for her mother and wanted to let go of those extra responsibilities. Now Libby knew Milly would be safe, have company during those long and cold winter nights, and no longer need to drive.

Milly was not happy about moving so soon, though she was less resistant than she had been a few months earlier. Libby helped her mother organize her thoughts and her possessions: "Which pieces of furniture, art objects, and other belongings do you want to take with you? Which do you want to give away to relatives and friends? Which do you want to sell or give to charity?" When she got right down to the task of packing boxes, Milly seemed to enjoy preparing for her move.

After packing and cleaning all day, Libby went to sleep in the guest room of the house that had been Milly's home for thirty years. Her mother, now a small and frail woman, usually rational and nonvolatile, came right up to the bed where Libby was sleeping and started to speak loudly: "You are forcing me out of my own home. You are making me do this." Libby sat up in bed and responded with great concern: "I hear how hard this move is for you. I am sorry you are unhappy, but I believe this the best choice for you at this time in your life. I will go with you tomorrow and help you unpack, and I will visit you often in your new home."

As Libby walked her mother back to bed, Milly gave Libby a hug. "Thank you so much—even for helping me move," she said.

Libby was able to help her mother make the transition into a senior residence by eliciting her opinions, involving her in the decision-making process, and respecting her feelings at the moment of moving. She did not tell Milly how to feel or act. She acknowledged the difficulty of the change. Milly felt heard, and Libby and Milly were able to support each other during the moments of emotional upheaval.

What Is Happening to This Body of Mine?

As Wanda began to lose weight and become weak from bone cancer, a home health aide suggested to Wade, her husband, that they make the bathroom safer with hand rails and a raised toilet seat. Wanda's three children were having trouble figuring out which of their parents was not following through on the aide's suggestion.

Was it Wanda or Wade who did not want these signs of decline around them all day long? They both had said they were going to make the changes, but then nothing happened. After a few weeks, their middle son, Earl, said he would buy and install the necessary items. Wade supported him; he wanted the increased safety for Wanda. He knew they would give her some comfort. He also took Earl aside and told him that Wanda was trying to get him to wait. To her, the changes in the bathroom meant the end was near. And why make the house look like it was set up for an old person when Wade would be selling it soon enough?

Earl did not know how to intervene. He called his friend Nan, a social worker. She advised Earl to tell his mother that he realized she did not want these things, and that he could well understand why—the look, the resale value of the house, the reminder that she was not going to live forever. Nan said he might even tell his mother that he worried about her. He definitely needed to be very respectful and loving about what was for his mother a major issue. In the end, Nan said, Earl should plead with Wanda to allow him to make the bathroom safer—for his sake. For her son, of course Wanda relented. Earl let his mother know he had heard her reluctance. Wanda felt heard by Earl and could then listen to him with an open mind and heart.

What if Wanda had stubbornly refused to allow the changes? When a parent refuses to accept the decline in her ability to care for herself, how hard should her loved ones push back? The parent's health and safety *and* the relationship with the parent need to be cared for. How can both be preserved with dignity? If Wanda had resisted the changes, should Earl have just ignored her?

In a difficult case, perhaps each member of the family needs to address the situation separately and quietly with the resisting person so she does not lose face or feel ganged up on and pushed into a corner. Each person—siblings, adult children, friends—can say the kinds of things that Earl said. The repetition might bear fruit. Here are some possibilities:

- I think this must be a difficult time in life for you.
- I think when I am unstable on my feet, I will resist the visible signs of aging—safety bars in the bathtub, a shower chair, and raised toilet seat.
- I worry about you. I want you to be safe.
- What are your plans for keeping yourself safe?

In a loving relationship, respect, self-direction, and, finally, acceptance all play a part.

Should I Invite My Mother to Live with Us?

As Sharon grew older, her daughter Angie worried about her more and more. Alone in her apartment, Sharon could fall and not be able to get help. She might be alone for days in bad weather. She might get no phone calls for a week. With her husband Arnold's consent, Angie decided to bring her mother to live with them. They remodeled part of the ground floor so she would have an easily accessible suite with a private bathroom. Sharon contributed some money from the sale of her house and moved in.

Angie soon found being with her mother after a day at work to be difficult. After all day alone in a strange house with no friends and nowhere to go, Sharon would complain and complain. Angie was unable to just listen. She wanted her mother to thank her for bringing her to her house, or at least not be so negative at the end of the day.

Angie and Arnold found that if Arnold visited with Sharon while Angie made dinner, the complaints never came out. Sharon would listen to Arnold and delight in everything he told her about his day. He got a kick out of spending this time with her. By the time dinner was served, the remainder of the evening went well as they sat together reading, watching TV, and chatting before going into their separate suites. Angie and Arnold learned to go upstairs as soon as Sharon went to her room so they could have some time alone. Soon Sharon also recognized their need for some privacy and at times purposely went to her room to watch her TV.

Sharon relayed this story to me, and admitted that initially she did not think she was complaining. She felt that Angie should have known everything that was going on with her. Arnold was nice enough, but she did not feel very comfortable with him. Then she learned to ask him about his day. She learned about his very complex business, which she had thought she would never understand, and she learned about his friends at work. She learned why her daughter loved this man. She looked forward to their little visits in the evening. He was quite entertaining and did not get impatient with her, as Angie did.

Arnold eventually learned that Sharon's memories of her childhood were quite interesting. He encouraged her to talk about her upbringing and about her years as a mother of young children. Mother's appreciation of Angie had long been a part of their conversations. With Arnold's encouragement, Sharon learned to speak directly to Angie about her gratitude.

Arnold suggested that Sharon try the following:

- Greet Angie with pleasure at the end of the day.
- Thank Angie for dinner and compliment her on what she liked about the meal.
- Occasionally thank Angie for inviting her into Angie and Arnold's home.

These complimentary remarks from Sharon made Angie more receptive to the complaints because they were balanced by her mother's satisfaction with the arrangement. Arriving to a place of comfort for each of the three members of this family took time and attention. Arnold needed to recognize how he could help and then, using his new relationship with his mother-in-law, coach her to compliment Angie. Ultimately, when Sharon came into the kitchen for dinner after spending time with Arnold, she was in a good mood, and the three became very comfortable living together.

How Do I Tell Someone I Love That Her Memory Is Failing?

Eliza and Beverly were sisters. They were both school counselors, they lived in the same city, they spoke on the phone a few times a week, and they often lunched together. They were very close. As Eliza approached seventy-five and was still working, Beverly noted that Eliza's memory was failing. Beverly suspected that Eliza was no longer capable of doing her work. For several weeks she carefully watch Eliza and listened to her responses in conversation. Beverly realized she had to say something to her sister—better that she say something than have the school board force her to retire.

Beverly carefully thought about what she should say, and came up with the following:

- I have to speak to you today about something serious.
- I speak to you with love and appreciation for all you mean to me.
- I don't want my concern in any way to interfere with our love for each other.
- I *note* [neutral word] that your memory is not what it used to be.
- You used to have a most amazing memory.
- Now I fear you are no longer capable of doing your work.
- I am sorry to be the one to say this to you, but I think you can hear it from me.

- I encourage you to think about what I am saying, resign, and enjoy your life.
- I want you to know I love and care about you.

At first Eliza felt shaken by these words, then she felt angry with Beverly. She did not feel ready for this life change. She did not like being seen as too forgetful to work. She also feared more serious losses to come. She thought long and hard about what Beverly had said. She did not talk with Beverly as often nor as openly during her weeklong internal debate. Finally Eliza began to test the retirement idea and come to terms with Beverly's advice. As she grew more comfortable with the idea of stopping work, Eliza was able to thank her sister for her honesty and to resign from her job. Only later was Eliza able to thank Beverly for speaking to her with love, not judgment.

How Do I Talk to a Person with Alzheimer's Disease?

Alzheimer's disease is going to affect more and more of us as more people live longer. Conversations among family members when one of them begins to experience memory loss become more challenging and difficult. The ability to perform the simple acts of daily living become more and more compromised. Decisions made one day may not be remembered the next day. Plans and facts need to be stated over and over. Helping loved ones take their medications and go to their appointments becomes necessary

Naomi's mother, mother-in-law, and father all had Alzheimer's disease by the end of their lives so she was well aware of the amount of patience needed to treat them with kindness. Naomi's mother, Nanette, knew the importance of being "oriented in both time and space," so when they were together, Nanette would repeatedly ask: "Where are we now? What day is it? Which route are we taking?

Do we have enough gas?" A few minutes later she would ask the same questions. Naomi would begin calmly, answering in an ordinary voice, concerned for how difficult being disoriented must be for Nanette. But as the day progressed, Naomi would become annoyed, wanting an end to the questions. She found herself resentful and not wanting to answer Nanette's questions, and then she would berate herself for her impatience. Finally Naomi learned to say:

- I know you can't help asking the same questions.
- I am sorry I am so testy with you.
- I would like to be more patient, but I am not.
- Please forgive me.

Just saying these few words relieved the pressure building up in Naomi and for a time she could return to her kinder self.

Naomi discovered that when she asked Nanette questions about the past or shared memories of their early times as a family, her mother was much more able to remember and participate in the conversation. Naomi did not correct any of her mother's mistakes regarding names or dates or facts; nor did she argue when her mother insisted Naomi hadn't told her things she knew she had told her. Instead she learned to enjoy her mother's stories and the time they spent together.

Because of Naomi's patience and appreciation for the decline that comes with age and Alzheimer's, she learned to approach each encounter with quiet love and devotion. The forgetting is not intentional, she knew. The forgetting will happen, she knew. Letting go of her attachment to having Nanette be her old self allowed Naomi to remain calm and appreciate what could still be shared between them.

When Should I Write My Will?

Each of us will handle our will, plans for our funeral, and make decisions regarding the disposition of our jewels and treasured objects in a very different way. "I have cancelled my appointment with my lawyer three times," a woman with cancer told a group I was leading. "I have been sitting on my half-finished will for six months," said another. "I am not ready for this," said a third.

I met a woman whose work includes being present when the terms of a will are drawn up by all members of the family—while everyone is still alive. She helps with the challenging decisions of what to give in-law children if they are predeceased by a hereditary child; how to plan for grandchildren when one child has four children and another child has none; and how to plan for grandchildren before and after they turn twenty-one.

Working with adult children to set terms of inheritance that are understood and agreeable to all family members is an important step in preparing them for your death. Why should a will remain a mystery until after the funeral? Families able to calmly converse with you about the distribution of your assets will have an easier time than trying to sort out your affairs during their time of grieving. Let your adult children know the results of your careful consideration, and then ask for their reactions to the information. Let them know that you have tried your best to be fair, and that the most important thing is to maintain harmony in the family.

A person who facilitates family meetings to discuss wills told me about a family in which the older son had made a great deal of money and the younger son was a struggling artist. In this case, the facilitator opened the conversation with a question to the two sons: "What has your thinking been on this subject?" The wealthy son responded, with his wife's agreement, that the split should be two-thirds of the estate to the younger brother, and one-third to his children, who were the only grandchildren. This was the result everyone else had hoped for, but having the suggestion come from the financially successful older son was far better than having it come from the parents. The forthcoming style of the older son saved that family a difficult conversation.

Making decisions about the distribution of property is not always this easy. What might parents ask in a family with dissimilar economic situations and no up-front offer by the wealthy sibling? Some of the questions that follow might help:

- We want to talk to you about our will.
- We are aware that each of you has a very different lifestyle.
- We want to be fair to all of you.
- We want to give you what we can to help you in the future.
- We want to dispose of our assets so that family harmony continues.
- We have been giving to you unevenly during our lifetime according to your needs.
- After our death, we would like the money to be divided equally. [Or, we have decided that we will divide our money unevenly at death.]
- We want you to know this now so we can discuss allocations that we all think are fair.
- How do these arrangements sit with you?
- We will talk about this again soon, after you have had time to reflect.

To make adult children feel a part of the process, even though the will is already written, some parents may decide to tell their children about the decisions that were troublesome. Other parents reveal all the terms of the will and let the children know that further discussions are welcomed. Children may find questioning any of their parents' decisions very difficult. How can children ask for more than has been given? Parents can encourage their children to think about all the eventualities that have been raised and maybe some that have not been considered. The goal is to lay a solid ground for future harmony by offering children an opportunity to be involved in decisions while stating out loud the desire that their relationships not be disrupted over money.

How Am I Going to Make Decisions for My Father?

All during his lifetime, Rodney had mood swings. In his sixties, he began taking mood-regulating drugs, and he became more predictable, pleasanter to his family, and gentler with his wife. This improvement was a great relief to everyone in the family. However, twenty years later, after his wife died, he stopped taking his medication. He became depressed. He was not getting up in the morning. He was not caring for himself or keeping his house clean. His four children—Steve, the oldest; Burt, the second; Ruth, the third; and Christopher, the youngest—were divided as to what to do. Steve wanted to hire a person to come in and care for their father. Burt did not want to spend the money. Ruth thought her father should be in a psychiatric hospital where his medication could be closely regulated. Christopher, still angry with his father for the negative treatment he had received as a child, thought they should leave him in his house to stay in bed all day. While the siblings argued, Rodney got worse.

Finally, the four siblings agreed that Rodney was a danger to himself and had him admitted to a psychiatric hospital. Rodney was furious. After thirty days on medication, he was stabilized and returned home, but he began to decline again after a few months at home. Rodney claimed he did not need his medication. The children feared that living alone he would become physically ill, fall, or lapse into a delusional state that could lead him anywhere.

They again agreed that Rodney needed to be in a state hospital. Burt, who lived the closest, called 911. There was no money for any other arrangement. Rodney's Social Security income paid the small monthly mortgage payments on his house and the utilities, with a little left for food.

During the next two years, Rodney rotated in and out of the hospital several times and both his physical and mental state continued to decline. He was fed well when he was in the hospital, but at home he did not eat. Now ninety, he was absentminded as well as depressed. His children seemed at a loss regarding what to do next when Steve decided to ask his father what *he* thought they should do. He waited until close to the end of a hospital stay, when his father was usually more alert and less volatile than at other times. Steve reviewed with Rodney what had been going on for the previous two years: Rodney had been going off his medicine, going into the hospital, getting stabilized, returning home, and then neglecting to care for himself. "What do you think is the best long-term plan?" he asked his father. The other children had been afraid to ask this question. They all thought Rodney might want to come and live with one of them, and no one was willing to consider this possibility.

Rodney dodged the question. He puttered around his room, making odd noises. Steve left. The next time Steve came to visit, he asked the same question and again got no response. On his third try Steve outlined for Rodney the options: stay home, take your meds, and take care of yourself; arrange for a Medicare aide to come to your house three times a week to clean up and oversee your medication; or go to a Medicare-approved residential center that specializes in care for people with your difficulties.

Rodney responded this time, saying that he might jump off a cliff. Undeterred, Steve said he was not sleeping nights worrying about his father. A decision had to be made. He did not want to continue hospitalizing Rodney every few months and having to drive more than a hundred miles each way to visit. Steve began to show his annoyance, which was new for him. Rodney finally paid attention.

Sometimes anger, used sparingly, can be useful, especially when speaking one's own truth with the intention of reaching a reasonable solution. Steve was in his sixties at this point, and this was the first time Rodney had faced his son's anger.

"I need you to make this decision," Steve told him loudly and firmly. "I can't tell you what to do. I will help you and support you when you pull together a reasonable plan. The hospital does not want you to use them as a fallback drop-in center."

Rodney looked down. "I can't make a decision," he said. "I can't think things through anymore."

Steve was stunned. He had not expected such an honest response from his father. Steve said, "Well then, I think your best bet is to move into a senior residence near all of us, where we can visit you and you will have the care you need. If you are concerned about your house, we can sell it and you will have that money for your new residence. We will make sure there is enough."

Rodney sat with these words, and when he was ready, he responded. "This is nearly unbearable. I need your mother and I don't have her. Just push me, help me, and I will go."

Rodney was not able to say thank you. Steve was not able to say thank you. The process had been painful for both of them. They had reached out to each other as far as they could. Each breathed a sigh of relief. They had done the best they could. Steve took over and began to make inquiries about various senior residences.

How Should I Make Decisions
When My Loved One Is Unresponsive?

As Shawn was terminally ill and nearing the end of his life, his children, Pam and Patrick, began to fight about whether or not he should be sent to the hospital with his next infection. Shawn's quality of life was very low. He was in bed all day, often sleeping, and when he was awake, he experienced a lot of pain. Shawn did not answer questions about his care and what he wanted. Pam wanted him kept alive at all costs. Patrick wanted his father to be left alone, without medical intervention, so he could die at home without a lot of useless procedures on his failing body. Pam and Patrick were locked in the last of a lifetime of battles. Each felt they were being more loving to their father.

Because Shawn left no written instructions, his children were locked in an unresolvable dispute. From this they each learned that they would talk to their loved ones well before death, when they were not yet sick, and discuss what they might want in various eventualities, then they would put the decision in writing for their loved ones and their doctor. Shawn finally died quietly in his sleep, in his bed, in his home, without any signal to call in medical assistance.

I have used the dying process of others as a means to talk to my adult children about what I want when I am dying. I try to imagine various states of pain and debilitation that would lead me to say, "No more interventions." I have a great sense of relief knowing that my children are aware of and support my hopes and intentions.

How One Family Let Mother
Go into Death

Gina's family was having a difficult time facing the fact that she was dying. They all wanted her to live. She was not yet eighty and in the midst of important historical research. Her grandson's wedding was approaching. They wanted her to live so badly that they were angry at her doctors for missing certain signs and not responding sooner to others. The infection around her heart could have been treated a week earlier and then maybe the fluid in her lungs would not have built up. They never talked to Gina about her impending death. They just kept doing all they could to keep her alive.

Gina became more and more lonely. She knew she was dying, but everyone around her was so cheerful that she felt isolated and denied. Finally she raised the questions on her mind with Peggy, her daughter-in-law: "Why is everyone so happy? Are my children aware I am going to die? What is happening here?"

Peggy explained that the family cried in the living room together, trying to protect her. They were all terribly frightened. Gina spoke to her doctor about the situation, who said he would talk to the family, but he never did. Finally Peggy called her local hospice for advice. A hospice counselor was able to encourage everyone to start talking before it was too late. The conversation began with one simple question: "What do you think is happening here?" The counselor looked to the patriarch of the family, Gina's husband, for the first answer. He went into his active, fixing, thinking mode, and focused on medical procedures and prognoses. Then the counselor asked for Gina's answer. She said simply, "I am dying." The whole tone in the room shifted. People shuffled, looked down, looked away, then looked at Gina and each other. Tears filled their eyes. They grew quiet inside for the first time in a month.

"How can each of us help you to die?" asked the hospice counselor.

"Visit me when you can. Tell me about your lives. Please, no more fixing, no more doctors, no more drugs, except to keep me comfortable. Let me talk about dying. Let me say goodbye to each of you. I love you all so much."

Each family member switched into simply spending as much time with Gina as possible. They talked about their sweet memories of times with her. They told her how much they loved and appreciated her for her understanding, her patience, her intelligence, and her sweetness. One son asked her to send him a sign if she were to discover an afterlife.

Some asked for forgiveness if they had ever hurt her. Gina asked forgiveness for anything she had done to hurt her children or her husband.

Gina and an old friend made up after many years of petty bickering. Friends murmured their goodbyes each time they left Gina's bedside, knowing they might not see her again.

All expressed their love over and over.

Soon Gina decided to stop eating and drinking. A rotation of hospice workers supported the family through the few difficult days while Gina was taking her leave. All family members took turns holding her hand and putting salve on her lips. They got on the bed and held her. They helped each other refrain from giving her water even when, in her semiconscious state, she asked for it. And then she slipped off. She missed the wedding. She left the research to others to finish. After saying goodbye to her loved ones, she had a peaceful exit. The friends and family who had the privilege of being with Gina during the last few days of her life were grateful to each other and to Gina for the openness, truth, and love that had been expressed.

Conclusion

At the end of life, people facing death take stock of who they are and how they want to be remembered. Whether a time of mellowing, a time of withdrawal, or a time of anger and regret, this is when relationships can be mended, apologies made, forgiveness offered. For those who die slowly and consciously, or who are with their loved ones when they die, this can be a time of opening to love, a time to give care and receive care. What a perfect time to appreciate what was good, to be grateful for the time that is left, and to prepare to let go into death. The family dynamics will not always be easy, painless, or pleasant. For those who are left, this can be a time for learning, and for the person leaving, a time for letting go. Great changes and shifts can take place when one member of a family or circle of friends departs from this life.

Afterword

I have come to believe that I have a warm heart-center within me where my love for others resides. That feeling in my heart has continuity beyond my behavior, my disagreements, and my moods. With the intimate loving connection of souls, difficulties can fall like dead leaves in a stream and wash away, leaving us standing strong and equal in the flow of life, ready to steady each other through whatever comes.

I believe that each of us can make the world better with small acts of kindness. By speaking without blame, revenge, retribution, jealousy, or anger, we can contribute to our world. Each day we can be mindful of what we are saying and the impact we might have on others. As we move toward candor and love with our intimate family members, so can we move out into the world with candor and love, bringing peace and harmony to ourselves and all beings.

—*Susan Halpern*

About the Author

Susan P. Halpern, MSW, has been a social worker and psychotherapist for more than thirty years. Her first book, *The Etiquette of Illness,* was excerpted in *O, The Oprah Magazine.* Halpern, who has three children and six grandchildren, lives in Berkeley, California, with her husband.